REPUBLICS OF THE NEW WORLD

Republics of the New World

THE REVOLUTIONARY POLITICAL EXPERIMENT IN NINETEENTH-CENTURY LATIN AMERICA

Hilda Sabato

PRINCETON UNIVERSITY PRESS

PRINCETON & OXFORD

Copyright © 2018 by Princeton University Press

Published by Princeton University Press,
41 William Street, Princeton, New Jersey 08540

In the United Kingdom: Princeton University Press,
6 Oxford Street, Woodstock, Oxfordshire OX20 1TR

press.princeton.edu

Cover image: "South America." Lionel Pincus and Princess Firyal Map Division,
The New York Public Library. New York Public Library Digital Collections.

All Rights Reserved

Library of Congress Control Number 2017954508
First paperback printing, 2021
Paper ISBN 978-0-691-22730-6
Cloth ISBN 978-0-691-16144-0

British Library Cataloging-in-Publication Data is available

This book has been composed in Miller

Para Julián y Andrés

CONTENTS

ACKNOWLEDGMENTS

MANY YEARS AGO, when I began to work on nineteenth-century Argentine politics, I soon realized that it was hard to think of the problems I faced without considering them as part of the larger history of the demise of the Spanish empire and the formation of the Latin American republics. From then on, my specific studies on Argentina were informed by that process and by its rich historiography, as well as by the debates on republicanism and political modernity beyond our region. Soon, and somewhat on the side of my focalized research, I started to delve more systematically into that history, until it caught my whole attention and finally inspired this book. This is a long story for a rather short essay, but it took time to come about and along the way I contracted innumerable intellectual debts, so many that any efforts on my part to do them justice will surely prove lacking. Let me try, nevertheless, to acknowledge those more directly connected with the writing of this book.

In my attempts to go beyond my limited field of expertise, I sought the aid and advice of colleagues who generously provided me with ideas, suggestions, and critical comments, as well as with specific references to published and unpublished works. My special thanks to Víctor Hugo Acuña, José Antonio Aguilar Rivera, Cristóbal Aljovín, Alfredo Ávila, Catalina Banko, Rossana Barragán, Ana Frega, Pilar González Bernaldo, Nils Jacobsen, Annick Lemperière, Carmen McEvoy, Cecilia Méndez, Luis Ortega, Juan Luis Ossa, Marco Pamplona, Erika Pani, Eduardo Posada Carbó, Natalia Sobrevilla, and Ana María Stuven.

[X] ACKNOWLEDGMENTS

But it was only through my years-long ongoing intellectual dialogue with friends and colleagues at home that I could conceive of and develop the main arguments of this book. I am particularly indebted to Natalio Botana, Paula Alonso, Beatriz Bragoni, Gabriel Entín, Noemí Goldman, Juan Carlos Korol, Eduardo Míguez, Elías Palti, Juan Carlos Torre, and Eduardo Zimmermann, as well as the members of our current seminar group at the University of Buenos Aires—Laura Cucchi, Leonardo Hirsch, Flavia Macías, María José Navajas, Inés Rojkind, Ana Romero, Jimena Tcherbbis Testa, Nahuel Victorero, and Ignacio Zubizarreta. With Marcela Ternavasio, we have spent long hours sharing questions and concerns regarding the present and the past, including among them most of the issues raised by this book. I thank her for her support and encouragement as well as for her sharp comments to the original manuscript. Above all, I remain forever in debt to Tulio Halperin Donghi, who inspired so many of my questions on Latin American history.

Crucial inputs to my work also came from discussion in seminars where I presented some the main arguments later developed here, at the following institutions: Université de Paris I, Emory University, the University of Georgia, Universidade de São Paulo, Foro Iberoideas, Pontificia Universidade Católica do Rio de Janeiro, 3° Congresso Internacional do PRONEX (Rio de Janeiro), the Davis Seminar at Princeton University, the Annenberg Seminar at the University of Pennsylvania, University of South Carolina, Freie Universität Berlin, and Universität Leipzig. My thanks to all those who participated in those sessions for their insights and comments, particularly to Jeremy Adelman, Tom Bender, Roberto Breña, Vera Candiani, Miguel Centeno, Oscar Chamosa, Roger Chartier, Linda Colley, José Murilo de Carvalho, Arcadio Díaz Quiñones, Miriam Dolhnikoff, Don Doyle, Antonio Feros, Paul Friedland, Barbara Göbel, Jürgen Kocka, Carlos Marichal, Stephanie McCurry, Hans-Jürgen Puhle, Bernardo Ricupero, Michael Riekenberg, Stefan Rinke, Daniel Rodgers, and Stanley Stein. My special thanks to Jeremy Adelman and Linda Colley who encouraged me to develop my sketchy manuscript into a full-fledged book and to Brigitta van Rheinberg, of Princeton University Press, who showed confidence in that possibility and subtly guided me in the ensuing process. The anonymous readers of PUP provided very useful suggestions and comments that helped me improve the original version.

I worked on this book in Buenos Aires and Cortaderas (Argentina) as well as in Berlin and Princeton. My gratitude to the institutions that supported me in this endeavor: the Programa de Estudios de Historia Económica y Social Americana (PEHESA) of the Instituto Ravignani, which belongs jointly to the University of Buenos Aires and CONICET; the Davis Center at the History Department of Princeton University; and the Lateinamerika-Institut at the Freie Universität Berlin. Also, to the librarians and archivists who kindly helped me in my searches through the three libraries that proved invaluable for my work: Firestone in Princeton, the Iberoamerikanische Institut in Berlin, and the library at the Instituto Ravignani in Buenos Aires. Federico García Blaya, in turn, assisted me with great efficiency in the collection and processing of information. In the course of my research, I received decisive financial support through grants from the University of Buenos Aires, CONICET, and the Agencia Nacional para la Promoción Científica y Tecnológica in Argentina, as well as through a Davis Center fellowship at Princeton University and the Humboldt Forschungspreis granted in 2012 by the Humboldt Stiftung in Germany.

In dedicating this book to my sons, Julián and Andrés Reboratti, I wish to express my deepest appreciation for the love and support I receive from them, as well as from their spouses, Loli and Nadia, and my endearing granddaughters Renata, Antonia, and Juana. Most of all, I thank Charly, my husband, for his good humor, his patience, and his loving care.

REPUBLICS OF THE NEW WORLD

Introduction

A GREAT POLITICAL commotion marked the beginning of the nineteenth century across the Spanish empire. Napoleon's occupation of the Iberian Peninsula shattered imperial unity and inaugurated a long history of political change on both sides of the Atlantic. In the Americas, most of the former colonial territories entered into a period of reformulation of the colonial links that ended in independence, followed by a vast, lengthy, and intricate process of redefinition of sovereignties and formation of new polities. Attempts at nation building followed different directions, and many a project was tried and failed, while no linear or predetermined path led to the fifteen individual nation-states in place by the end of the second half of that century.

There was, however, a common denominator to that complex process: the polities in the making, the short- and the long-lived alike, all adopted forms of government based on the principle of popular sovereignty. Spanish America was, therefore, part of the larger history that involved the English, the American, and the French revolutions, the foundation of constitutional monarchies, the invention of a federal republic in the United States and of other republican regimes in Europe, and—above all—the institution of the sovereignty of the people as a founding principle of the political. These developments shattered the edifice of the ancien régime in various parts of the world where, from then on, the political no longer referred to a transcendent instance but was considered a human construct. The making of the Spanish American republics belongs to this broader picture. Until a short while ago, however, this experience remained marginal to the mainstream narratives of political modernity that revolved around the northern Europe-United States axis. By introducing Spanish America into this story of political transformation, this book joins the work of other scholars who, in recent years, have adopted a more global approach in order to widen the scope of those narratives.

Popular sovereignty marked the way to modernity, but within that framework two main regime options were available: the constitutional monarchy and the republic. At a time when most of the Western modern polities endorsed the former, the Americas, both North and South, and with the sole exception of Brazil, opted for the republic. There was no single republican model, and the label applies to a wide variety of ventures across the continent, but all of them entailed a radical innovation in the ways of instituting the polity and of legitimating authority. If the former Spanish territories were not original in their move toward popular sovereignty, their adoption of republican formulas tried on a vast scale was unparalleled outside the United States, and it inaugurated a decades-long history of political experimentation in the ways of the republic. The purpose of this book is to reflect upon this vast and long-term "republican experiment"[1] in Spanish America as part of the broader political transformations experienced during the nineteenth century in a global context. It also seeks to illuminate that larger process under a new light, and thus contribute to reshape the overall history of republics and republicanism.

The Adventure of Self-Government

By the mid-1820s, all of continental Spanish America had left behind the colonial condition and entered into a new political era, marked by the adoption of popular sovereignty as the founding principle of the polity and of the republic as the favored form of government. This implied a radical change at the level of what Pierre Rosanvallon has called "the political," that is, "the modality of existence of life in common,"[2] a change that in this case meant a complex transit from a social order consisting of natural or God-made communities and corporations that integrated the body of the kingdom to a secular, nontranscendent, man-made, self-instituted polity. This transit was not a straight road, but rather a winding path of irregular trajectory and unpredictable ending. Nevertheless, the decisions—that proved final—to replace the divine right of kings and to dismiss the constitutional monarchy alternative set the stage for the new, that is, for the successive experiences in republican self-government. Yet these experiences were themselves subject to the uncertainties and tensions of a self-instituted "life in common," which triggered an open-ended process for decades to come.

The founders of the new polities faced two main challenges. First, how to reconstruct political authority on the bases of popular sovereignty. This was both a theoretical and a very practical matter that, throughout most of the century, found various, always partial, solutions. Second, how to define the human and territorial contours of the polities that were to be the sources of that sovereign power as well as the domains for its application. The severance of the colonial bond had led to the formal erasure of the old territorial division characteristic of the imperial institutional arrangements. Yet the initial proposals to create a single "nation" did not prosper, and the following decades witnessed the drafting and redrafting of new boundaries, and therefore, the shaping and reshaping of the polities. The vicissitudes of this story owed as much to the colonial legacy as to the challenges of the postcolonial era, and their traces were still visible in the relatively stable pattern of republics-cum-nations that crystallized by the second half of the nineteenth century.

The focus of this book relates to the first of these questions, that is, to the problem of the creation and legitimation of political authority in Spanish America. The adoption of republican forms of government entailed a radical change in the foundations of power and the "invention of the people"—to borrow the term used by Edmund Morgan in his seminal book on Britain and the United States.[3] Besides this simple yet indispensable initial platform, there were no fixed formats or universal protocols that defined a republic, so that actual republics could and did vary greatly throughout the century.

Despite this variability, and the social, economic, and cultural diversity of the Spanish American territories, the polities that took shape across its variegated geography show common patterns and trends of political organization that defined a distinct republican order that lasted for more than five decades. This order was in flux, but it revolved around certain recognizable principles and institutions common to most of these republics until roughly the 1870s. The problems they had to face were often similar, as were some of the directions they followed to solve them. They also found common inspiration in the available republican examples and ideological traditions.

In their initial drive toward self-government, the postindependence leaderships were well aware of the broader connections of local events, and were committed to what they perceived as the larger struggle on behalf of modernity. They were also strongly influenced by the political traditions and developments beyond the region. The United States featured in a prominent place, but other historical cases appealed in various ways to the founding fathers and their successors: the classical republics—particularly Rome—the Italian early modern city-states, the United Provinces of the Netherlands (late sixteenth to late seventeenth century), and revolutionary France, plus the prestigious English constitutional monarchy and the short liberal experiences in Spain (1812, and 1820 to 1823). These external examples remained a source of reference for the rest of the century, together with a widespread awareness of the Brazilian case—a neighbor constitutional monarchy subject to both praises and critique. But the locals did not mimic any of the existing models; rather, they adapted and innovated, adopted or rejected external influences according to their own legacies and experiences. In short, they followed their own ways, and although criticism ran high in certain periods and places, the search for solutions to the actual political problems did not lead them to fundamentally challenge the republic. Unlike what happened in several European cases that opted out of their republican regimes, Spanish Americans stuck to them for good.

In their search for inspiration in the ways of the republic, they also resorted to the available pool of changing ideas and values in circulation. They could find it in the republicanism of the ancients and in the more recent forms of eighteenth- and nineteenth-century French and Italian republican thought or of Anglo Saxon civic humanism, as well as in the various and successive formulations of what came to be known as "liberalism." Also, they could turn to the doctrine of natural rights, from Grotius to Vattel, and to different strands of the Catholic tradition. The echoes of socialist thinkers reverberated in several places after the midcentury, when also positivism gained an increasing presence in most of the region. These ideological lineages provided a shared background whose elements were usually combined in very eclectic ways, shaping original political languages whose main concepts were strongly rooted in the current political contexts.

This changing repertoire provided different and sometimes conflicting orientations for the formulation and reformulation of norms, institutions, and practices that shaped the political life of the republics. Yet innovations in this regard resulted mainly from the concrete political experience of self-government, which turned out to be a risky undertaking with unpredictable effects. In that context, contemporaries sought different ways to produce and reproduce power and authority within the framework of the republic. They tried various normative and institutional alternatives, and devised mechanisms to channel the participation of the "sovereign people"—whose definition was itself controversial. This process of experimentation resulted from a combination of very conscious exercises in innovation and the unpredictable effects of political action, so that the consequences usually went well beyond the wishes and expectations of the main actors of the political game.

By the midcentury, most of the nations-in-the-making had established certain institutional and normative thresholds devised to stabilize the political system, such as the affirmation of individual rights and freedoms, the regulation of government powers, and the explicit demarcation of citizenship. For most of the period, however, political life remained highly volatile. Instability, in fact, proved to be an inbred feature of these republican regimes—as we shall see throughout this book. And although concerns regarding the difficulties to achieve a more predictable political order were commonplace, only by the last decades of the century did they amount to an overall challenge to the prevailing republican values and practices, which led to decisive changes in the rules of the game and inaugurated a new political era that best fitted in the dawning global age of nationalism and imperialism.

Points of Departure

Scholars have long discussed the characteristics of nineteenth-century Spanish American politics. For years, they considered its pervasive volatility as a symptom of the "failed" modernization of the new polities, where liberalism could not set foot on account of different factors, from colonial heritage to premodern forms of resistance. This literature produced some of the more compelling interpretations of the Latin American past that are still persuasive and highly influential. In recent years, however, historians are leaving behind the teleological perspectives that informed those views, and rather than seek to measure the actual history of the area in terms of the liberal canon, or try to detect obstacles presumably obstructing the road to progress, they are now exploring how politics actually functioned then and there. Liberalism itself has been revisited, as well as the conventional narratives of its all-encompassing influence in the construction of political modernity in the United States and other Western nations. No longer considered to be an exception, Latin American political history is understood in its own terms and as part of that wider story. From this fresh angle, the issue of the instability of nineteenth-century politics may be addressed anew as part of the history of the republic, not only in Spanish America.

Recent scholarship has also left behind a second powerful view of that history, which considered nineteenth-century politics exclusively as an elite affair that kept the rest of the population aside or barely included on the margins. Historians now claim, to the contrary, that the shaping of the Spanish American republics involved not just elites and would-be elites; it implicated larger sectors of the population in politically significant forms of organization and action. It has shown how people from different walks of life mobilized in large numbers and became involved in the political life of the new polities in the making. In this regard, Spanish America shares some of the main traits of political modernization in other areas, while at the same time it shows specific features that account for the intensity of its politics during most of the nineteenth century.

This vibrant scholarship is my point of departure.[4] Latin American historiography has profited immensely from the recent revival and renovation of political history. In the last twenty to thirty years, the number of books, articles, and dissertations in the field has been larger than all the earlier production put together. This expanding corpus has succeeded in changing our former views of politics and the political in nineteenth-century Latin America. The studies cover a wider range of topics, regions, and periods; they display various methodological perspectives and put forward different interpretations. Most of them deal with national, regional, or local cases, although there is an increasing tendency to include transnational comparisons not just within Latin America but also considering other areas of the world.

I also rely heavily on the theoretical and historical scholarship that studies republicanism, citizenship, the public sphere, revolutions, and more generally, nineteenth-century politics beyond Spanish America. This literature has also offered new concepts and insights in the last decades, and it has allowed me to think the problems I am concerned with in comparative perspective. Moreover, this study has given me the opportunity to deploy theoretical and empirical inputs that come from different sources and combine them in order to make sense of the overall republican experience.

Itinerary

In the light of these theoretical and historiographical references, this book explores what I have called "the republican experiment" by delving into a crucial component of politics in the republics: the relationship between people and government that developed after the adoption of popular sovereignty as a founding principle of power. While most of the current literature is concerned with particular countries or regions, and chooses to focus either on the elites and would-be-elites or on the popular classes (in some formulations, the "subaltern"), this book points to the common traits and shared tendencies in the relationships established *between* "the many and the few" across Spanish America in the period of the 1820s to 1870s.

In order to reflect upon how power and authority were redefined in the republican era, I seek the commonalities among very different societies through a long period of time; therefore, the differences—which of course are many—are concealed or minimized. Moreover, not all areas of Spanish America are equally covered by the existing literature, so that my interpretations are surely biased in the direction of the countries most favored by it. In this regard, I have decided to limit my arguments to continental Spanish America, thus leaving aside the islands of the Caribbean, which offer a rather different trajectory.

The chosen time span, in turn, has allowed me to conflate these experiences, as it leaves behind the highly conflictive and heterogeneous processes of independence to concentrate on the core decades of the republican thrust, and ends when that thrust waned in the face of new formulas and actions toward the consolidation of nation-states. For roughly five decades after independence, I find a shared pattern in the ways of the republic, particularly as regards the main topic of this book.

The people were at the center of the adventure of self-government, so a great part of the history of the new republics is tied to the ways in which this abstract principle was made effective in the institution and reproduction of the polity. And the people are also at the center of this book, but rather than attempting an overall consideration of this multidimensional object, I follow a more limited approach and focus primarily on the normative frameworks, institutional setups, and actual practices involving the people of the Spanish American republics from the 1820s to the 1870s. Three dimensions of the political life of the period offer a privileged point of entry to explore that relationship: elections, armed citizenship and the militia, and "public opinion." These by no means exhaust the possible ways of addressing the chosen topic, but they were spheres of political discourse and action crucial to the forging of politics in the republics. Therefore, the central part of this book explores how these instances worked as arenas for the definition, action, and representation of the people, as well as for the construction and legitimation of power. From there, I go on to discuss the formation of the modern polity, the changing contours of citizenship, the dynamics of politics, and other key features of the Spanish American republican experiment from the aftermath of independence to the last decades of the century. In connecting these developments to the global context and particularly to other republican experiences, I hope to illuminate that larger history from a fresh perspective.

Chapter 1 presents the Latin American scenario at the time of the imperial crisis that plunged the former colonies of Spain and Portugal into a succession of events with unforeseen consequences. There is a very rich literature that discusses Napoleon's occupation of the Iberian Peninsula in the context of the struggles for domination among the main European powers, as well as its multiple consequences for the Iberian empires both at home and overseas. With this historiographical background, the chapter focuses on the final outcome for the American mainland territories under imperial rule: their independence from their metropolis and the subsequent disputes around conflicting sovereignties. Secondly, it discusses the available options of political organization after the severance of the colonial bond, and the choices made in this regard, which led Spanish America in the republican path while Brazil became a constitutional monarchy. The challenges posed by the adoption of republican forms of self-government are at the center of the rest of this chapter, which focuses on the attempts at reconstructing political power on the basis of popular sovereignty and on the final controversial decision to introduce modern representation as the appropriate way to create legitimate authority. This decision opened the way to the definition of different dimensions of political citizenship that will be the main theme of the following three chapters.

Chapter 2 revolves around one of the key mechanisms devised to materialize representation: regular elections. Suffrage, elections, and electoral practices are discussed here in tune with a vast recent scholarship on this subject that has radically changed the former prevailing views on the right to vote and the role of elections both in the dynamics of political struggle and in the relationships between "the many and the few." The Spanish American record and performance in such matters were not very different from those of other contemporary republics; if anything, and contrary to conventional wisdom, the former reveal more systematic widespread electoral participation than was the case in most west European countries. The right of suffrage was widely extended among the male population, and although not all potential voters actually attended the polls, those who did came from a wide social spectrum. Electoral machines, in turn, show striking similarities all over the Atlantic world, where partisan organization and competition often set the pace of practical politics. Despite the controversies often raised around Spanish American elections, for most of the period, these were the main legitimate road to government posts, and they offer a key to understand the politics of the republic.

As the ultimate source of power, the people were not only in charge of electing governments but also of controlling them regularly. While the periodical exercise of the suffrage could be considered a means of checking chosen representatives, the regular control of those elected rested mainly in the hands of public opinion, on the one side, and of the citizens in arms, on the other. Chapter 3 focuses on the latter. Today we are familiar with the role of the former in our democracies, but armed citizenship is no longer mentioned as a valid means of keeping government power in check. For most of the nineteenth century, however, it was an important aspect of republican regimes—not only in Spanish America.

As guardians of popular sovereignty, citizens had the right and the obligation to defend freedom and to bear arms in the face of any abuses of power. Although this was an individual right, its effective exercise was channeled through the institution of the militia. The chapter analyzes the creation and transformation of the militia—in its different formats, including the national guard—as well as its relationships with the professional army. It discusses the fragmentation of military power, and the role both institutions played in politics. As the material incarnation of armed citizenship, the militia was considered a genuine political player; it intervened in times of elections and performed important functions in the civic rituals of the republic. Above all, it was a decisive player in revolutions. The use of force was deemed legitimate against abuses of government power, so that revolutions (in various forms) became a regular and frequent means to challenge the existing authorities on the charge of alleged despotism. This chapter ends with a discussion of this distinctive form of political action. In contrast with a long scholarly tradition of considering revolutions as a typically Spanish American premodern form of resistance, I argue that they were part and parcel of the new, of the practices developed during the era of the republic, not only in this part of the world.

Public opinion is the focus of chapter 4. The adoption of popular sovereignty and representative government introduced a dimension to politics that was increasingly referred to as "public opinion," the voice of the people that was to exert control over those in power. This concept was widely used at the time, and it had changing meanings, but it was central to the republican rhetoric and procedures of the nineteenth century. This chapter concentrates on the institutions and practices connected to public opinion, such as the periodical press, the associative movement, and other instances of public action. The study of the Spanish American case adds new insights to the current theoretical and historical debates around Habermas's theory of *Öffentlichkeit*, and provides new evidence for exploring the ways in which civil and political society articulated in republican contexts.

The last chapter puts together the different dimensions explored in the previous three, and advances an interpretation of the shaping of the Spanish American republics, with focus on the relationships between the people and government, and the boundaries of inclusion in and exclusion from the polity. The introduction of popular sovereignty and the adoption of republican forms of government changed the scale of politics, and it opened the way to the development of a vigorous political life that involved large sectors of the population in the creation and legitimation of power. The chapter first concentrates on the two protagonists of republican politics, the "ruling few" and the "many," and refers to their respective collective profiles and the main venues of political involvement, as well as to the transformations thereof. It then goes on to discuss the creation and development of partisan formal and informal networks that articulated participation through elaborate material and symbolic means and gave shape to a highly inclusive yet unequal and strongly hierarchical political life. Competition and conflict were the engines of politics, whose internal dynamics—I argue—was marked by an inborn instability, fueled by republican values and practices. For decades, this feature did not get in the way of the legitimacy of the system, which proved quite efficient in shaping authority and delivering political rule. In the last quarter of the century, however, this prevailing order entered into a critical phase, and the chapter finishes with an overview of the incoming changes that led the way to the political novelties of the fin de siècle.

Finally, a short epilogue reflects on some of the main trends of the nineteenth-century republican experiment in Spanish America in the context of the overall history of modern republics.

Landscape

At the time of independence, the territories that had been part of the Spanish empire in the Americas had many things in common. For starters: three hundred years under the same colonial rule, which meant the social organization under the premises of a corporate and hierarchical society of orders, the political subordination to the rules of the absolute Spanish monarchy, and the economic dependence upon the imperial needs. Also, they were all under the cultural and spiritual determinant power of the Catholic Church, which had strong economic and social connotations. But there were also many differences among those territories, from the geographical settings to the resource endowment, the population size and composition, and the actual social structure. Even certain features that may seem analogous at first sight soon reveal their disparities. Such is the case, for example, of the multiethnic configuration of the population that was common to all areas, but had, at the same time, marked regional differences. Thus, at the heart of the Andean region as well as in central Mexico, over 60 percent of the population was classified as indigenous—itself a highly heterogeneous category—a figure that was much lower in the Southern Cone as well as in Colombia, Venezuela, and parts of Central America. Blacks—most of them slaves—were strongly represented in the areas around the Caribbean basin and in some parts of the Pacific coast. The numbers of mestizos and mulattoes was also variable, as was the figure for "blancos."

The imperial crisis brought about decisive changes in Spanish America. First of all, there was large-scale war: more than fifteen years of armed confrontations—not only against Spanish domination but also to solve internal conflicts—all of which dislocated the established economic and social organization. The severance of the colonial bond further affected the previous order, so that by the aftermath of independence, the former Spanish territories in America had entered a new era. There was, in the first place, the radical innovation in the political sphere discussed above and in the rest of this book. There was, also, a succession of territorial rearrangements and, for several decades, the actual boundaries of the polities in the

MAP 1. Spanish America: Political division circa 1800

making were in flux (see maps 1, 2, and 3). The economy, in turn, experienced an important reorientation due to the end of the colonial demands and restrictions, which meant the redefinition of internal circuits as well as the opening up to the international markets. Changes in the social and cultural

MAP 2. Spanish America: Political division circa 1830

landscapes happened more gradually, and colonial legacies coexisted with the new values, institutions, and practices for decades to come.

The impact of these developments varied greatly across Spanish America, so that the nations already defined by mid-

MAP 3. Spanish America: Political division circa 1900

century showed significant differences in their social and economic structures, which came even more visible in the following decades. All of these countries increased their connections with the world market and their dependence toward the financial and commercial dominating powers thereof—first among them, England. They produced primary goods for export, and imported most of the manufactures and the capital required for growth. But this equation varied greatly according to the resource endowment, the structure of production, and the size of the internal markets, among other factors, so that, for example, countries like Argentina and Colombia could better profit from the situation than others with less favorable conditions, like Bolivia. Nevertheless, all of them experienced the vulnerability of their dependent condition and subordinate place in the world economy.

The social landscape was also diverse. By the end of the nineteenth century, population size ranged from over twelve million in Mexico to around two to four million in Argentina, Chile, Colombia, Peru, and Venezuela, to below two million in the rest (Bolivia, Ecuador, Costa Rica, El Salvador, Guatemala, Honduras, Nicaragua, Paraguay, and Uruguay). Areas with strong European immigration, such as Argentina and Uruguay, had experienced the highest rates of growth, while the rest had more or less multiplied their population by two to three in sixty years. An increasing process of *mestizaje* contributed to modify the ethnic profiles of most countries, which nevertheless kept their initial basic patterns. The early eradication of the colonial caste system did not erase the many deeply ingrained forms of discrimination against indigenous peoples, while the dismantling of slavery took several decades with initial steps to stop the trade and free the newborn, with abolition usually coming later.

Most of the people lived in the countryside, and although urbanization accelerated in the last decades of the century, the majority of Spanish Americans qualified as rural residents. These were mostly illiterate peasants or workers employed in low-skilled jobs. Literacy rates were higher in the towns and cities, where schooling expanded after the midcentury, together with jobs in manufacturing and the service sector that required certain qualifications on the part of the salaried labor force and the self-employed. Unskilled hands were still an important presence among urban workers, a fact that increased the differentiation within the popular classes. The expansion of a middling sector was characteristic of late nineteenth-century cities and in some rural areas, a feature that was more significant in some countries than in others.

Spanish American societies were strongly hierarchical, but the sharp distinction between the so-called *gente decente* or *hombres de bien*—a vague denomination that connoted possession of material assets and symbolic capital—and the plebeian rest, typical of the first half of the century, gave way to a newly stratified social structure. The image of an overall concentration of wealth and economic power in the hands of a small and closed class of powerful families may apply to some specific cases and periods, but in many others—and especially in the larger countries—it fails to account for the dynamism of these societies where the powerful one day could be successfully challenged the next. Within the context of a nonlinear transition from a basically traditional mercantile structure of production to one increasingly marked by capitalism, the upper classes were subject to the risks and hazards posed by the new demands of the system. This transformation did not diminish or eliminate social difference; on the contrary, it opened the way to a renewed process of stratification legitimized by the new creed of individual self-realization and the ideology of personal progress, typical of the fin de siècle.

By then, little was left of the Spanish America that broke its ties with the empire. We may even doubt of the pertinence of conflating this whole area with its fifteen different, very heterogeneous nations in a single collective. So why does this book wade into such dubious waters? In this case, I made the choice at the end of the road, when I realized how much of what I thought specific of the political history of Argentina was actually part of a larger story, one that led me beyond its frontiers to the transnational scene. While trying to make sense of the local in a global context, I found more: that the nineteenth-century political developments in the River Plate belonged to the Spanish American experience of the republic and to the wider history of political modernity. So it is to that experience that this book now turns.

CHAPTER ONE

New Republics at Play

The passages from empire to nationhood forked in ways that required actors to make choices without knowing the certainty of the outcome.

—ADELMAN (2006), 1

AT THE BEGINNING of the nineteenth century, Spanish America was part of the larger three-centuries-old empire built by the Spanish monarchy across the Atlantic. By the late 1820s, most of this territory was no longer under imperial rule; it was in the midst of a transformation that no one then knew—as Jeremy Adelman perceptively remarks in the above cited quote—where it would lead or how it would result. With the advantage of hindsight, we know that by the end of that century fifteen nation-states were in place. No linear or predestined path, however, led from empire to nations, and very much like in other parts of the world, the transition from colonies to independent states was a complex, conflict-ridden, indeterminate process. Narratives of nation building have often portrayed this story as that of the progressive road that, despite many obstacles and difficulties, inevitably led to a happy ending, that of the formation of a new, independent, nation. These views are now subject to heavy criticism, as recent scholarship has produced a whole new set of hypotheses and interpretations on the fall of empires, the history of colonialism, and the formation of nation-states. In the case of Spanish America, teleological narratives of national developments have been displaced by highly elaborate analyses of the different courses followed by the former colonies as they severed their links to the metropolis and sought to shape new polities. Also, historians have eroded the long-standing claims that independence from Spain was the result of an inward liberating energy in each of the future nations-to-be; rather, the crisis of the Spanish monarchy and Napoleon's invasion of the peninsula was at the core of the ensuing disbanding of the empire.

There is a vast scholarship on those topics that explores and discusses the occupation of the Iberian Peninsula by the French forces in the context of the struggle for power among the main European countries, as well as its multiple consequences for the Spanish and the Portuguese empires at home and overseas. Although the resulting literature provides an indispensable background for this book, in the following pages I will only refer to some of the main arguments and conclusions regarding the final outcome for the American mainland territories under imperial rule: their independence from the metropolis and the ensuing conflicts around the definition of new sovereignties, as well as to the disputes and the choices made regarding the available options for political organization after the severance of the colonial bond.

A Critical Turning Point

The facts are well known. In the midst of intense rivalries among the European powers, and with Napoleon's France on the move to subdue the Iberian empires, in 1808 an internal dispute within the Spanish royal family that resulted in the displacement of King Charles IV and the crowning of his son, Ferdinand VII, opened the way to the invasion and occupation of the peninsula by a powerful French army, and finally, to the abdication of the novel king replaced by Napoleon's brother, Joseph (as José I). The demise of the Bourbons triggered the spark for a political process of unforeseen consequences. The king was, by definition, literally the head of the body politic, and the whole edifice of the Spanish monarchy was built upon that principle. Sovereignty was at stake. The uprooting of the legitimate sovereign set off a succession of reactions both in the Peninsula and in the Americas, as different parts of the composite body of the Spanish realm claimed to resume the powers originally bestowed upon their king.

In Spain, local juntas in various places led the resistance against French forces, guerrilla warfare spread all over the territory, and intense political and ideological debates pitted different sectors of the fragmented leadership against each other. Successive attempts at concentrating power on a central authority culminated in the creation of a Supreme Central Junta, formed by delegates from each of the main local juntas, and designated to rule in the name and place of the king. First established in Aranjuez, the Junta was forced to move to Seville, and at the end of 1809, under pressure from the French, to flee to Cádiz where a local rebellion compelled its resignation and the delegation of its authority to a Regency council created in early 1810. Despite the relentless advance of the occupiers, the locals managed to sustain their authority in the southern port of Cádiz, where that same year they convened the Cortes, an assembly meant to represent the whole of the Spanish body politic, which two years later produced a liberal-oriented constitution, a radical novelty in the tradition of the kingdom.

These efforts notwithstanding, the French ruled over most of the country. The Spanish rebels were no match for the formidable French army, and it was only when the English came in as allies of the Portuguese to stop Napoleon in Portugal and the Russian campaign forced the emperor to pull out part of his troops from Spain that the occupation came to an end. In 1814 Ferdinand VII was restored to the throne. In the context of a strong revival of absolutism in Europe, the Spanish king gained the support of most powers, including dominant England, and sought to return to the ways of the Old Regime.

In the meantime, nothing remained the same in America. The power vacuum sparked by the king's abdication reached the colonies as soon as the news traveled that far. The first reaction headed by local Spanish authorities was to condemn the invaders and confirm fidelity to their displaced king, rejecting all appeals on the part of José I to shift their loyalties. But the question of sovereignty came up soon enough; in the absence of the head, the body parts of the realm, that is, the provinces, "kingdoms," or "pueblos," very much like in the Peninsula, started to claim back the sovereign powers once vested upon their monarch. The efforts of the Bourbon administrations, since the beginning of the eighteenth century, to discipline the kingdom and its colonies under their centralized absolutist authority found their limits in the new situation, on both sides of the Atlantic. The old doctrine and traditions that considered the monarchy a composite of bodies, cities, corporations, and kingdoms resurfaced in the midst of the crisis. This revival soon shared the political and ideological stage with other, more recent theories regarding sovereignty and power also opposed to absolutism and to the divine right of kings. All over the empire, the reality of an empty throne set off heated intellectual debates and fierce political disputes, in the midst of a multi-sided display of force, of revolutions and wars that did not end with the restoration of Ferdinand in 1814 but lasted for another ten years.

In an attempt to rein in their imperial possessions, the metropolitan authorities reached out to the American colonies and convened them, in 1809, to choose their own representatives to the Junta Central, a move that opened up an unprecedented electoral process and at the same time fueled debates and claims regarding the place of these territories in the realm. By the time those elections were decided in part of Spanish America, the Junta was dissolved, so that the representatives never joined that body. The colonies were entirely immersed in the quagmire of events shattering the empire, and when the news arrived of the fall of Seville and the forced resignation of the central Junta, uncertainty escalated, authority crumbled, and conflict openly broke out among different groups around sovereignty and power. In various cities across the colonial territory, the locals proceeded to convene their own juntas in the name of the people entitled to recover their sovereignty, just as the provinces had done in Spain. This move had precedents in 1808 and 1809 when similar bodies assembled, with different claims and outcomes, in Mexico, Montevideo, Quito, and Upper Peru,[1] but in 1810 it acquired new intensity and, starting in Caracas and Buenos Aires, expanded throughout the colonial territories. Colonial officers in place lost their role as legitimate authorities, and only the local municipal bodies, the Cabildos, maintained and enhanced their representative character, while the juntas proclaimed their sovereign powers.

Sovereignty

The colonies were in turmoil, well beyond the control of empire. From that point onward, the former territorial units under Spanish rule—viceroyalties and *capitanías generales*, but also their different parts—entered into a disjointed period of political fragmentation, each of them following a different, often irregular course whose only common denominator was the pervasive immersion in war.

The 1810 revolutionary claim to self-rule was a widespread starting point, but it came in different formats and opened up a vast field for divergence. Apart from the full-fledged reaction against that principle on the part of those in favor of absolutism, two were the main controversial issues at stake: the nature of the new sovereign and the quality of the relationship with the metropolis.

Scholars have long discussed the ideological foundations of the Spanish American claims to self-rule. In recent years, the prevailing views have pointed in the direction of two, noncontradictory, directions: the neoscholastic doctrines and the theory of natural rights, both of which informed the political languages that circulated in Spain and its colonies. The former recovered the principles of the so-called ancient constitution of the Spanish monarchy, prevalent in the times of the Habsburgs but displaced by the Bourbons' shift toward absolutism. According to its main tenets, sovereignty originally pertained to the various corporate, organic, "natural"—God created—bodies that bequeathed their original powers granted by God in the person of the king, and remained linked to him by the mutual commitments of their *pactum subjectionis*. The king's *imperium* was not unconditional, and under special circumstances, sovereignty could revert to its initial holders. Such was the claim put forward by the provinces in Spain and the colonial territories on occasion of the *vacatio regis* that followed the French occupation: in the absence of the monarch, the "pueblos" (original communities) recovered their sovereignty.

This proposition found a second source of validation in various theoretical formulations—in circulation since the seventeenth century—based upon the doctrine of natural rights, all of which had conceptual connections with neo-scholasticism but at the same time responded to a different set of notions regarding power and society. As regards the question of sovereignty, the main innovation was the rejection of transcendence in favor of the contractual nature of human association. As a result of the pact that had brought them together, men as individuals created their own authorities to whom they transferred, by consent, their sovereign powers. Relations between government and the governed were ruled by the key principle of consent, and therefore, legitimate authority was never absolute, it was always subject to the control of the people. This principle was formulated not only by the classic names associated with the updating of the theory of natural rights (Gropius, Puffendorf, Wolff, Vattel) but was also part of the political philosophy of John Locke and other founders of liberal thought. It had entered into the vocabulary of the Atlantic revolutions that preceded the Spanish American ones and was openly put forward in the declaration of independence of the United States.

Regardless of the specific theoretical frameworks to which they initially belonged, these notions served to back the claims to self-rule both in Spain and its colonies, and entered into the political languages in rapid transformation during the critical years of the imperial crisis. This was a time when available words did not match the needs of naming; contemporaries attributed novel meanings to old concepts and inserted them in new contexts, altering current languages and shaping new ones that often proved unstable. Sovereignty, with its various meanings, occupied center stage in all of them, so that conflicts regarding authority and power were also disputes about meaning.

In this regard, a key divide would soon come up that proved highly consequential in the years to come: the question of plurality or unity of sovereignty, an issue that surfaced as soon as the first juntas were set up, as well as during the debates that preceded the sanctioning of the Cádiz constitution of 1812. The basic problem was whether the existing kingdom should recognize the plural nature of the realm and therefore grant sovereign powers to each of the natural communal bodies (*pueblos*, cities, provinces, "republics," and such) claiming self-rule or whether the kingdom (as a single "nation") should remain one and its people, as a unitary body, retain the powers once vested upon the monarch. After much debate, the Cortes settled on this second option and thus gave shape to a unified nation in which they included not only the metropolis but also the former colonies. This solution created a powerful antecedent for the disputes that were taking place in America, but the problem persisted, and for decades, the question of how far could the claim to self-rule go was not settled. In fact, in the years to come, in most of the former colonies the issue of competing territorial sovereignties remained one of the main causes of political conflict.

Independence

The second great field for controversy was the relationship of the former colonies to the metropolis. During the early years of the imperial crisis, as we have seen, among the leading sectors of the Spanish American societies there seemed to be a widespread inclination toward expressing loyalty to King Ferdinand and condemnation of the French invasion. In that context, the first steps to establish local juntas did not challenge the fundamental ties with empire; rather, they followed the metropolitan moves in the same direction. This initial consensus, shared by large sectors of the population, soon experienced the impact of the dramatic events in Spain. Starting in 1810, the succession of local movements pursuing self-rule followed new directions, and the issue of the colonial links acquired increasing relevance. The new juntas swore their loyalty to Ferdinand, but at the same time most of them questioned the legitimacy of the Regency council in Spain and of the colonial magistrates in place. Open conflict ensued. The metropolitan government censored these moves, the Spanish magistrates and officials in America insisted on their powers, different sectors of the political, social, and economic elites—which included Spanish-born and American-born "Spaniards"—realigned themselves in favor of or against the juntas' decisions, and in a short time, a deepening division between loyalists to imperial authorities and those now considered "insurgents" (or "patriots") split large sectors of the population who took sides in the conflict.[2] Among the many novelties of those years, the creation of an open public debate nurtured by a newly created press and the circulation of all sorts of rumors, together with the physical presence of sectors of the urban population in plazas and other common spaces, heated the political atmosphere in unprecedented ways.

The colonial relationship was under scrutiny. But downright declarations announcing the severance of the bonds with Spain did not prosper until later. The first formal statements in this regard were formulated by the juntas of Caracas and Cartagena, in 1811, but they were rather exceptional for the time being, and they proved ephemeral, as the loyalists rapidly regained control of those territories and restored them to metropolitan rule.

Talk about "independence" became, nevertheless, more and more audible, yet the term admitted different meanings. This word had acquired new valence after the thirteen North American colonies declared the severance of the "political bonds" with Great Britain, and their decision "to assume among the

powers of the earth, the separate and equal station to which
the Laws of Nature and of Nature's God entitle them." They
were thus pronouncing the "United colonies as Free and Independent states," and establishing their new status vis-à-vis the
rest of the nations of the world. In the context of the Spanish
empire, however, the word was used rather freely to refer to
various types of proposed arrangements in the relationship
with Spain. Thus, "independence" could, for example, denote
the affirmation of self-rule of territories that would nevertheless stay within the Spanish "nation" and loyal to the Crown; it
could refer to the aspiration of the subordinate regions of a
viceroyalty to gain an autonomous status within the colony;
and it could also carry the radical connotation of complete rupture that recalled the case of the United States.

This diversity of meanings somehow reflects the messy political realities of Spanish America. Every corner of the colonial
territories was in ferment, with political disputes developing
into armed confrontations of increasing virulence. "Insurgents"
gained the first rounds in the former viceroyalty of Nueva
Granada and the Capitanía General de Venezuela, as well as in
the River Plate and Chile. In other areas, loyalists prevailed.
But in all cases, uncertainty and instability were the rule, with
frequent shifts in the power positions and changes of fronts.
Moreover, each side had its own internal conflicts, so that war
often confronted those presumably under the same flag, a situation that has prompted some scholars to qualify these confla-
grations as "civil wars."

By 1814, the overall situation changed, when Napoleon's
forces left Spain, Ferdinand VII recovered the throne, and the
European powers openly endorsed his claims to reestablish
absolutism and regain control of the whole empire. To this
end, the king decided to send a powerful army across the Atlantic, to enlarge the existing loyal forces—mostly manned by

American-born recruits. Despite the financial difficulties of the kingdom, the years that followed witnessed the advance of Spanish troops almost everywhere, together with the defeat and repression of insurgency. Two years later, only parts of the former Viceroyalty of the River Plate remained in the hands of the revolutionaries; the rest was almost completely under the control of the loyalists.

The revolutionary armies, nevertheless, continued their struggle. The so-called insurgents went a long way toward achieving the professionalization of their forces, and the coordination between them and the more informal guerrillas active in the fight against the loyal troops. The Spanish armies, in turn, advanced and occupied formerly insurgent areas at the price of intense repression, but success in gaining a massive favor of the locals often proved elusive. Financial stringencies further hampered the possibility of reinforcements from the metropolis, and attempts at recruiting a large new contingent to send to America failed miserably. In 1820, in the midst of increasing protests against the king, an uprising led by military figures ended in the fall of the absolutist government, the reinstallment of the Constitution of 1812 that established a constitutional monarchy, and the subordination of Ferdinand to the new situation. Loyalists in Spanish America found a new opportunity to demand a negotiated settlement of self-rule within the empire and under the liberal charter, a solution that did not satisfy the metropolis and found partial support only in Mexico, while the rest of the former colonies were already going in a very different direction.

In fact, the recovery of large territories by the loyalist was soon followed by the military and political reorganization of the patriots. Two large armies commanded by Generals San Martín and Bolívar advanced successfully from their original homes, in the River Plate area and New Granada/Venezuela respectively, to "liberate" (their term) the subcontinent. Success was slow in coming, but in the end, the Spanish were defeated. In New Spain, in turn, developments followed a rather different, more negotiated course. Nevertheless, and after more than ten years of struggle, all of the former colonies, at different moments during the decade-long wars (1814–24), had cut their bonds with Spain and declared total independence.

Self-Rule

Wars, however, were not the only concern of those who lived in the colonies. The *vacatio regis* left these territories without a legitimate authority, for—as we have seen—the solutions found in Spain to replace the absent king gained only partial support in the Americas. The option for self-rule was an answer to that critical situation, but far from solving the many problems raised by the power vacuum, it opened new questions and posed crucial dilemmas regarding how to rule these lands. Sovereignty was, again, the central issue.

The adoption of self-rule implied a radical challenge to the divine right of kings that informed the imperial order until 1808. The guiding principle indicated that sovereignty reverted to the people, which the new authorities presumably represented. But what people? According to the principles of the ancient constitution, the organic, "natural," corporate bodies of the monarchy resumed their original powers; in Spanish America, these were basically the concrete, territorially defined, communities—the *pueblos*, in plural—that had been distinguished by the Crown with certain privileges and obligations. In fact, the first juntas came to life in some of the main towns that enjoyed royal distinction, and they operated as incarnations of the God-created community. This view, as mentioned, coexisted with other, increasingly accepted notion of the people as an abstraction that referred to the sum of individuals, equal and free, who had originally entered the social pact and consented on being ruled by their own created authorities. In day-to-day political debates, documents, and decisions, contemporaries often overlapped these two different ways of understanding the sovereignty of the people, and although the first was tied to the imaginaries and realities of the ancien régime and the second one challenged such a representation of the polity, their discursive and practical coexistence marked the initial years of the crisis. The traditional worldview, however, was gradually, though not straightforwardly, undermined by the new ideas, which in practice meant the formal elimination of the corporate society in favor of a society of equals, free architects of their political community. The Cádiz constitution introduced important elements of the latter, while the examples of the United States, the English, and the French constitutions pointed more clearly in the same direction. The first Spanish American charters mostly followed those examples, but, as we shall see, this path opened yet more uncertainties.

A second challenge posed by the adoption of self-rule also refers to the problem of what people. The crisis of the colonial bond had not only contested the foundations of power; it also put into question the existing territorial divisions. When the first juntas claimed to rule in representation of "the people," it was not at all clear if they meant their town with its original jurisdiction as a corporate body, the sum of the individuals that inhabited the town and its hinterland, the larger territory they headed in the colonial order (the viceroyalty, the *intendencia*, and such), the aggregate of the Spanish American colonies, or any variant thereof. Territorial sovereignty was at stake. The multiplication of claims to self-rule bears witness to this conundrum. Juntas sprung in different corners, not just in the main towns that had enjoyed the favor of the Crown, but also in subordinate towns, villages, and communities, all of which talked in the name of the people, their own but also that of a whole area presumably under their control. The fragmentation of authority followed, as well as successive attempts at concentration, all of which bred conflict and war.[3] The Cádiz constitution sanctioned the unity of the Spanish "nation," both sides of the Atlantic, a proclamation that did not rein in the centrifugal tendencies that were dividing the American colonies. Whole areas were torn apart by juridical claims, political disputes, and military confrontations between those who favored the formation of new polities (nations) integrating different areas under a single centralized sovereign power and those who rejected all attempts at centralization in support of the autonomy of the different "pueblos" that could come together under political arrangements but without renouncing their own sovereignty. While the first of these positions would eventually have to face the problem of the external boundaries of each new nation, the latter had to deal with the question of how far could the demands for new sovereign territories go without falling into total fragmentation. In the end, all these dilemmas marked the transition from colonies to the new polities, and were not entirely solved until much later, several decades after independence.

Popular Sovereignty

In this conflictive and at times chaotic context of competing projects, powers, and forces, Spanish Americans had to face the problems posed by the revolutionary decision of adopting popular sovereignty as the founding principle of the polity and as the only source of legitimate power. This bold step was not without recent precedents, but the outcomes were far from reassuring. The French revolution itself provided a much-feared example of the dangers involved, while the Haitian case closer to home emerged as the nightmare the insurgent leadership dreaded the most. Republican United States as well as the English constitutional monarchy offered more moderate results, and despite the huge differences between their circumstances and those of the Spanish American colonies, they became sources of inspiration, together with other examples more distant in time.

The establishment of a new order of things required, so the current trends indicated, the sanctioning of a constitution, the pact that founded the new polity and at the same time invented the rules according to which it would function. England, revolutionary France, the United States, and Spain during its liberal sprees, all had their constitutions. Napoleon, in fact, insisted on granting such charters to conquered lands, destined to replace the institutions of the Old Regime and impose his own version of the modern, under the tutelage of France. At the time of the imperial crisis, the Spanish Americans resorted to that novel practice and sought to found and regulate their new sovereign spaces through constitutional means, as well as through other, less ambitious statutes and declarations.

As early as 1811, the *juntista* movement in New Granada produced a series of constitutions drafted in several localities that proclaimed their right to self-government, such as Cundinamarca, Santa Fé de Bogotá, Antioquia, Tunja, Popayán, among others. Venezuela witnessed a similar process. The conflict of interests among different levels of the territorial organization (municipalities, provinces, the viceroyalty) found a juridical solution in confederate schemes that articulated the different sovereign units into a loose association that gave some sort of unity to an otherwise fragmented space. These arrangements were ephemeral; internal struggles, loyalists' expansion, and the reconquest of New Granada and Venezuela by the Spanish armies, marked the end of this first constitutional moment.

During the same decade, other areas of Spanish America also sought to sanction and regulate new forms of association and government, and followed the constitutional path, usually with short-lived success. More consistent results came after the successive declarations of independence from 1816 onward, and by the mid-1820s, the constitutional wave had reached almost all corners of the former colonies.

All these documents, despite their great differences, shared a basic set of principles the revolutionary leaderships favored. Sovereignty of the people—with all its ambiguities—was universally proclaimed, together with a contractual notion of the polity mainly inspired by the more modern formulations of the doctrine of natural rights. Security, freedom, and equality were basic inalienable rights of all individuals belonging to the polity, and the juridical hierarchies upon which the Old Regime society of orders (and castes) rested were to be dismantled. Although these structures proved resilient, the language of modern constitutionalism prevalent in the experiences of the revolutionary age permeated the constitutions of this period and inspired important steps toward the institution of the new polities.

A key question addressed by these initial experiments was that of the form of government. The affirmation of self-rule based upon the sovereignty of the people did not provide a unique answer to that question, nor to the problem of how to create, validate, and reproduce legitimate power and shape political authority. In very general terms, after the rejection of any theologically grounded version of the foundations of power, the current favorite options were basically limited to constitutional monarchy and republic, although both these forms in turn

came in different shapes. During the turbulent period between
1810 and 1824, the two were proposed at different times, and
republican inclinations prevalent among the first insurgent
groups were challenged by those in favor of constitutional
monarchy, particularly after the European powers, in their
conservative post-Napoleonic mood, showed their preference
for the latter and reluctance to support what they considered
dangerous republican tendencies. The Spanish reestablishment of the Cádiz constitution and the Brazilian choice for
independence under a constitutional monarch pushed further
in the same direction. In Mexico, independence in 1821 came
together with the institution of an emperor, Agustin I, and in
other places, like Peru and the River Plate, initiatives to establish that type of regime led to rather desperate searches of
heads to crown—among European princes, among noble lineages of the indigenous groups, and others. Also, inclination
for constitutional monarchy prevailed in the Spanish American
territories under loyalist control where (and when) the Cádiz
constitution held force.

The Republican Way

All these schemes, however, as Rafael Rojas persuasively argues in his book *Las repúblicas de aire*, were left behind and
the republic became the final option in all of Spanish America,
a choice that proved wide-ranging and long-lasting. Talks and
writings favoring the republic circulated early on in the century, but explicit constitutional endorsement was less frequent.
Again, New Granada offers the initial examples, as the State of
Tunja constitution of 1811 was the first one in the Hispanic
world to openly define itself as such, and with the only exception of Cundinamarca's monarchical option, all the others followed suit. In these early cases, strong inclination for the re-

public often coexisted with less radical versions, which considered that form of government adequate at the local level but did not rule out the possibility of accepting Ferdinand back as king of the whole Spanish "nation."

Final independence did not necessarily come together with the republican option, but in the last years of the decade of 1810, the prevailing mood started to shift in that direction, which was finally explicitly acknowledged in the constitutions of the 1820s: the Republic of Colombia (comprising the territories of New Granada, Venezuela, and Quito) in 1819/21; Peru in 1823; Mexico in 1824; República Federal de Centroamérica (comprising the provinces of Guatemala, El Salvador, Honduras, Costa Rica, and Nicaragua) in 1824; Bolivia in 1825; the River Plate provinces in 1826; Chile in 1828; Uruguay in 1829. Paraguay, in turn, had established its own peculiar republican regime in 1811. After 1830, in continental Spanish America, the republic was there to stay, and with the sole exception of Mexico in the years of the French invasion and the empire of Maximilian (1864–67), it remained the overall chosen form of government for the rest of the century and beyond.

There was, however, no single republican model, and the label applied to very different actual regimes, some of them short-lived, others more lasting, all of them prone to recurrent legitimacy crises that often bred political instability and demands for change. This volatility, however, did not lead to any fundamental challenges to the republican principles such as those that cut short similar experiences in nineteenth-century Europe—for example, in France, Italy, and Spain. Despite the difficulties they encountered, Spanish Americans stuck to their original option.

In the 1820s this option was inspired by the already existing republics, as well as by the historical precedents and the Spanish traditions. The political and intellectual elites were well aware of what went on in the rest of the Western world, and of the successful and failed examples of republics in history. They were also concerned about the ways in which the colonial heritage could interfere with the revolutionary plans to eradicate the edifice of the Old Regime and shape these societies anew. But the troubles they soon had to face were not just the result of the past; in fact, the construction of the novel republics was fraught with problems that also stemmed from the innovations involved in the self-institution of the new polities.

The constitutions of the 1820s could not settle the problem of territorial sovereignties raised after the severance of the colonial bonds, which had resulted in debates around the shape of the future nations as well as in open conflict among different parts of the liberated areas. Independence had not only put into question the foundations of power, it had also erased the old territorial divisions. The geographical limits of the new polities were an open matter, and there followed a long period of drafting and redrafting of boundaries. Initially, the colonial divisions held, but soon, there were proposals to reshape the political map of Spanish America. Ambitious continental plans like those put forward by Simón Bolívar to unite the former territories of the Spanish empire, which did not exclude the possibility of embracing Brazil and the islands of the Caribbean then under British and French rule, were soon replaced by geographically more limited experiments. By the 1820s, the constitutions show new arrangements, and while in the River Plate area the former viceroyalty ended up split into several republics, New Granada and Central America adopted a more consolidated pattern. This layout, however, proved rather short-lived, and the national landscape changed several times until it reached a more stable definition around the midcentury.

The early republics remained also torn apart by confrontation between central and local powers, and most attempts at concentrating authority at a center were met by strong claims on the part of different localities and regions in defense of their own share. In this matter, scale was an issue. In the past, republics had only survived in relatively small areas (the city-state being the favorite). In fact, the question of size had become a matter of debate early on in the United States and was finally solved through the imaginative invention of a new set of political institutions and rules devised to meet the challenge. In Spanish America, each republic-in-the-making faced the dilemma of concentrating or fragmenting authority, and different solutions, involving both negotiations and confrontations, were tried through the years. Three main models prevailed: the unitary republic, the federation (the Philadelphia formula), and the confederation. None of these were, however, clear from the start, and in all cases the disputes around these alternatives were at the center of the political life of the republics.

Government by the People

Regardless of their final territorial shape, each new polity faced the challenge of making operative the principle of popular sovereignty. In the past, republics had found different ways of solving that problem, from the direct presence of the people assembled to decide to the quite widespread system of selecting government officials by election, rotation, and lottery. In the late eighteenth century, these mechanisms were left behind, as the representative system was offered as a theoretical and practical solution to the rule of government by the people. Yet representation did not have antecedents in the republican traditions. Voting had been used before, but not in order to represent the many; it was just a practical mechanism to appoint magistrates and other officials, and it was often combined with lots (in Rome, in Venice, in Florence, among others) in order for chance to counteract the presumably aristocratic bend of elections.

In turn, representation found nonrepublican precedents in medieval and modern times when royal and ecclesiastical authorities convened parliaments, courts, and councils for consultation on measures that required the consent of the realm. The corporate bodies of the kingdom selected delegates that were to act in their name, and according to the instructions received from the electors, decide upon the matters that were submitted to their consideration. Thus, as Bernard Manin has convincingly argued, "at the time when representative government was established, medieval tradition and modern natural rights theories converged to make the consent and will of the governed the sole source of political legitimacy and obligation."[4]

This connection notwithstanding, modern representation implied a radical shift from the older forms. Representatives were no longer a counterweight to the power of the sovereign; they themselves embodied the sovereign power of the people in the modern nation. But it also differed from the republican traditions of self-government. With the end of the society of orders, the people—in singular—was conceived of as the abstract community formed by free, autonomous, and equal individuals, united by their own will. The social realities of a plurality of persons were therefore subsumed in the political equality that allowed for the institution of one people. While in the republican tradition the collective will was generated by the members of the polity (the citizens) assembled for that purpose, in the new era, citizens had no direct role in decision making now left to their representatives. Selected in periodical elections, they were to act for, and at the same time produce, the people's will.

The tension between the belief that power should stem directly from the people (an association of equals) and any operation whereby a selected few were set apart and designated to exert power in their name had run through the entire history of the republic, and had cast suspicion upon the different means to designate government officials. Representation did not overcome this dilemma, but it offered the solution of a combination of democratic and aristocratic means: elections by all to select the few. Nevertheless, the question of the relationship between the representatives and the represented remained an open matter—and it still is in our present-day democracies.

A second dilemma involved in representative government posed even more challenges to the republican projects of the revolutionary era. Representatives were chosen by individual citizens, embedded in their actual social conditions, but once elected they presumably represented the political community (the nation) as an indivisible whole, and they materialized the unity of the people. This quandary informed the debates around the unity or the plurality of the polity, an issue that permeated the discussions around the forms of representation and the heated controversies around the figure of the political party (see chapter 2).

Despite these difficulties, by the early nineteenth century those societies that had popular sovereignty as the instituting principle of their polity and the only source of legitimate power opted for representative government. This step did not go uncontested. In the era of revolution, direct democracy found advocates both sides of the Atlantic, and Spanish Americans were not an exception. In their case, moreover, the colonial institution of the Cabildo Abierto could be assimilated to a people's assembly, and it gained popularity in the new scenario.

At the same time, some features of the ancien régime forms of representation, like the imperative mandate, resurfaced and competed with the newer forms.

In this contested context, however, sooner rather than later the trend toward modern representative government prevailed. Mechanisms associated with direct democracy did not prosper, while those inherited from colonial times survived only in the margins. Elections, in turn, became the key procedure to ensure representation, and therefore, in the creation of authority and in the legitimation of political power. They were as well a crucial moment in the relationship between the people and government. The right to choose and to be chosen constituted the core of the political rights enjoyed by the members of the polity, the citizens.

As the ultimate source of power, the people were not only in charge of electing the government but also of exerting a regular control over it. The legitimacy of the voted authorities was highly dependent on how they were evaluated, judged, criticized, or praised during their terms in office. "Public opinion" played a decisive role in that respect. Bernard Manin has underlined the link between representative government and the freedom of public political opinion. He understands this freedom as a counterpart to the autonomy of the representatives who are not tied to their represented by any type of instructions or mandates; "it has the effect not only of bringing popular opinions to the attention of those who govern, but also of connecting the governed among themselves."[5]

This concept, widely used in eighteenth-century Europe to discuss the foundations of authority, soon migrated to Latin America where, in the early days after independence, the enlightened elites considered public opinion together with the suffrage as the basic pillars of political legitimacy. Although the specific meanings of "public opinion" changed greatly throughout the century, it was a driving force both in the establishment of certain civil liberties, such as the right to free speech and to associate, and in the creation of a series of institutions and practices that were to prove important in the political life of the period.

Furthermore, in order to avoid government "corruption" and "despotism," Spanish Americans introduced the citizens' right and obligation to bear arms. Within the framework of a lasting republican tradition, they recovered a colonial institution, the militia, now reoriented to national defense as well as to the protection of the republic. In principle, armed citizens were meant as guardians of popular sovereignty; in practice, the militia and its successor, the National Guard, became important political actors throughout most of the century. The literature on representation has paid little attention to the connection between representative government and the right of the citizens to arm themselves in defense of freedom. Yet the contemporaries counted resistance to tyranny among the natural rights of the people, which remained valid in the case of representative polities where those elected could fall into despotic practices and, therefore, become liable to the armed resistance of those who had initially chosen them for office.

Representative government, as we have seen, produced a split among equals and elevated a few to a position of power. Regular elections ensured that this procedure connected those few to the many, and periodically validated their place. At the same time, the introduction of "public opinion" and armed citizenship allowed for the sustained control of those elected, for the supervision of the ways in which they exercised actual power. Legitimacy of origin (elections) was thus complemented by legitimacy of exercise.

The following chapters will address these three instances in the relationship of people and government by exploring the main institutions and practices related to them: elections, armed citizenship, and public opinion.

References

Adelman, Jeremy. 2006. *Sovereignty and Revolution in the Iberian Atlantic.* Princeton, NJ: Princeton University Press.

———. 2015. "Una era de revoluciones imperiales." In González Bernaldo de Quirós, *Independencias iberoamericanas.*

Aguilar Rivera, José Antonio. 2000. *En pos de la quimera: Reflexiones sobre el experimento constitucional atlántico.* Mexico City: Centro de Investigaciones y Docencia Económicas y Fondo de Cultura Económica.

Aguilar Rivera, José Antonio, and Rafael Rojas, eds. 2002. *El republicanismo en Hispanoamérica: Ensayos de historia intelectual y política.* Mexico City: Centro de Investigaciones y Docencia Económicas y Fondo de Cultura Económica.

Aljovín de Losada, Cristóbal. 2000. *Caudillos y constituciones: Perú, 1821–1845.* Lima: Pontificia Universidad Católica del Perú; Mexico City: Fondo de Cultura Económica.

Annino, Antonio. 2015. "Revoluciones hispanoamericanas: Problemas y definiciones." In González Bernaldo de Quirós, *Independencias iberoamericanas.*

Annino, Antonio, Luis Castro Leiva, and François-Xavier Guerra, comps. 1994. *De los imperios a las naciones: Iberoamérica.* Zaragoza: IberCaja/Forum International des Sciences Humaines.

Annino, Antonio, and Marcela Ternavasio. 2012. "Crisis ibéricas y derroteros constitucionales." In Annino and Ternavasio, *El laboratorio constitucional iberoamericano.*

Annino, Antonio, and Marcela Ternavasio, eds. 2012. *El laboratorio constitucional iberoamericano: 1807/1808–1830.* Madrid: AHILA; Frankfurt am Main: Iberoamericana Vervuert.

Armitage, David, and Sanjay Subrahmanyam, eds. 2010. *The Age of Revolutions in Global Context, c. 1760–1840.* Houndmills, UK, and New York: Palgrave Macmillan.

Ávila, Alfredo. 2004. *Para la libertad: Los republicanos en tiempos del Imperio, 1821–1823.* Mexico City: Universidad Nacional Autónoma de México.

Bonilla, Heraclio, ed. 2012. *La Constitución de 1812 en Hispanoamérica y España.* Bogotá: Universidad Nacional de Colombia.

Botana, Natalio. 1994. "Las transformaciones del credo constitucional en Iberoamérica durante el siglo XIX." In Annino, Castro Leiva, and Guerra, *De los imperios.*

———. 2016. *Repúblicas y monarquías: La encrucijada de la independencia.* Buenos Aires: Edhasa.

Breña, Roberto. 2006. *El primer liberalismo español y los procesos de emanci-

pación de América, 1808-1824: Una revisión historiográfica del liberalismo español. Mexico City: El Colegio de México.

———. 2013. *El imperio de las circunstancias: Las independencias hispano-americanas y la revolución liberal española*. Mexico City: El Colegio de México; Madrid: Marcial Pons.

Breña, Roberto, ed. 2010. *En el umbral de las revoluciones hispánicas: El bienio, 1808-1810*. Mexico City: El Colegio de México; Madrid: Centro de Estudios Políticos y Constitucionales.

———. 2014. *Cádiz a debate: Actualidad, contexto y legado*. Mexico City: El Colegio de México.

Calderón, María Teresa, and Clément Thibaud, eds. 2006. *Las revoluciones en el mundo atlántico*. Bogotá: Universidad Externado de Colombia/Taurus.

Carrera Damas, Germán. 2010. *Colombia, 1821-1827: Aprender a edificar una República Moderna Liberal*. Caracas: Universidad Central de Venezuela/Academia Nacional de la Historia.

Chiaramonte, José Carlos. 2008. "Conceptos y lenguajes políticos en el mundo iberoamericano, 1750-1850." *Revista de Estudios Políticos* 140 (April/June) (Madrid).

———. 2010. *Fundamentos intelectuales y políticos de las independencias: Notas para una nueva historia intelectual de Iberoamérica*. Buenos Aires: Teseo/Instituto Ravignani.

Chiaramonti, Gabriella. 2012. "El primer constitucionalismo peruano: De Cádiz al primer Congreso Constituyente." In Annino and Ternavasio, *El laboratorio constitucional iberoamericano*.

Fontana, Biancamaria, ed. 1994. *The Invention of the Modern Republic*. Cambridge: Cambridge University Press.

Frasquet, Ivana. 2012. "Orígenes del primer constitucionalismo mexicano, 1810–1824." In Annino and Ternavasio, *El laboratorio constitucional iberoamericano*.

Frega, Ana. 2012. "Soberanía y orden en la Banda Oriental del Uruguay: Espacios de frontera y tiempos de revolución." In Annino and Ternavasio, *El laboratorio constitucional iberoamericano*.

Furet, François, and Mona Ozouf, eds. 1993. *Le siècle de l'avènement républicain*. Paris: Gallimard.

Goldman, Noemí. 2012. "Constitución y representación: El enigma del poder constituyente en el Río de la Plata, 1808-1830." In Annino and Ternavasio, *El laboratorio constitucional iberoamericano*.

Goldman, Noemí, ed. 2014. *Soberanía*. Vol. 2 of Javier Fernández Sebastián, dir., *Diccionario político y social del mundo iberoamericano*. Madrid: Universidad del País Vasco/Centro de Estudios Políticos y Constitucionales.

González Bernaldo de Quirós, Pilar, ed. 2015. *Independencias iberoamericanas: Nuevos problemas y aproximaciones*. Buenos Aires: Fondo de Cultura Económica.

Guerra, François-Xavier. 1992. *Modernidad e independencias*. Madrid: Mapfre.

———. 2000. "La identidad republicana en la época de la independencia." In *Museo, memoria y nación: Misión de los museos nacionales para los ciudadanos del futuro,* compiled by Gonzalo Sánchez Gómez. Bogotá: Ministerio de Cultura.

Guerrero Barón, Javier, comp. 2014. *La Constitución de Tunja de 1811 y la invención de las repúblicas latinoamericanas.* Tunja, Colombia: Universidad Pedagógica y Tecnológica de Colombia.

Halperin Donghi, Tulio. 1961. *Tradición política española e ideología revolucionaria de Mayo.* Buenos Aires: Eudeba.

———. 1985. *Reforma y disolución de los imperios ibéricos, 1750–1850.* Madrid: Alianza.

Irurozqui, Marta. 2012. "Huellas, testigos y testimonios constitucionales: De Charcas a Bolivia, 1810–1830." In Annino and Ternavasio, *El laboratorio constitucional iberoamericano.*

Lorente, Marta, and José M. Portillo Valdés, eds. 2012. *El momento gaditano: La constitución en el orbe hispánico (1808–1826).* Madrid: Cortes Generales.

Manin, Bernard. 1997. *The Principles of Representative Government.* Cambridge: Cambridge University Press.

Morelli, Federica. 2012. "De una Audiencia a múltiples Estados: El primer constitucionalismo ecuatoriano." In Annino and Ternavasio, *El laboratorio constitucional iberoamericano.*

Morgan, Edmund S. 1988. *Inventing the People: The Rise of Popular Sovereignty in England and America.* New York: W. W. Norton.

Palti, Elías J. 2007. *El tiempo de la política: El siglo XIX reconsiderado.* Buenos Aires: Siglo XXI editores.

Pocock, J.G.A. 1975. *The Machiavellian Moment: Florentine Political Thought and the Atlantic Republican Tradition.* Princeton, NJ: Princeton University Press.

Portillo Valdés, José M. 2006. *Crisis atlántica: Autonomía e independencia en la crisis de la monarquía hispana.* Madrid: Fundación Carolina/Marcial Pons.

Quintero, Inés, and Ángel Rafael Almarza. 2012. "Dos proyectos: Un solo territorio; Constitucionalismo, soberanía y representación, Venezuela 1808–1821." In Annino and Ternavasio, *El laboratorio constitucional iberoamericano.*

Rinke, Stefan. 2010. *Revolutionen in Lateinamerika: Wege in die Unabhängigkeit, 1760–1830.* Munich: Beck.

Rodríguez O., Jaime E. 1998. *The Independence of Spanish America.* Cambridge: Cambridge University Press.

Rodríguez O., Jaime E., ed. 2005. *The Divine Charter: Constitutionalism and Liberalism in Nineteenth-Century Mexico.* Lanham, MD: Rowman and Littlefield.

Rojas, Rafael. 2009. *Las repúblicas de aire: Utopía y desencanto en la revolución de Hispanoamérica.* Buenos Aires: Taurus.

Rosanvallon, Pierre. 1998. *Le peuple introuvable: Histoire de la représentation démocratique en France.* Paris: Gallimard.

———. 2003. *Pour une histoire conceptuelle du politique*. Paris, Éditions du Seuil.

Sabato, Hilda, and Marcela Ternavasio. 2015. "De las repúblicas rioplatenses a la República Argentina: Debates y dilemas sobre la cuestión democrática." In González Bernaldo de Quirós, *Independencias iberoamericanas*.

Stuven, Ana María. 2012. "De la autonomía a la república: El debate constitucional en Chile, 1808–1833." In Annino and Ternavasio, *El laboratorio constitucional iberoamericano*.

Stuven, Ana María, and Gabriel Cid. 2012. *Debates republicanos en Chile: Siglo XIX*. Vol. 1. Santiago de Chile: Ediciones Universidad Diego Portales.

Thibaud, Clément. 2012. "En busca de la república federal: El primer constitucionalismo en la Nueva Granada." In Annino and Ternavasio, *El laboratorio constitucional iberoamericano*.

Tuck, Richard. 2016. *The Sleeping Sovereign: The Invention of Modern Democracy*. Cambridge: Cambridge University Press.

Van Young, Eric. 2001. *The Other Rebellion: Popular Violence, Ideology, and the Mexican Struggle for Independence, 1810–1821*. Stanford, CA: Stanford University Press.

Zuckert, Michael P. 1994. *Natural Rights and the New Republicanism*. Princeton, NJ: Princeton University Press.

CHAPTER TWO

Elections

THE INTRODUCTION OF representative government was a
shared feature of the new republics in the making; the implementation of elections followed suit.[1] Even before the drafting
of the constitutions that were to regulate the structure and
functioning of governments, elections were held to designate
the authorities that replaced the colonial rulers. In the following decades, systems of government and political regimes varied greatly from place to place, but all of them included elections as a means to access and validate power.

In Spanish America there was some previous experience
regarding elections, in part originating in colonial times within
the corporate order of the ancien régime, and in part stemming
from the more recent practice of elections to the Spanish Cortes, during the critical years of the Napoleonic invasion of the
Peninsula—both before and after 1812, when the Cádiz liberal
constitution introduced modern representation into the imperial territories.[2] At the same time, the examples of other countries with more established electoral systems circulated widely
in the region, and, together with the Cádiz design, they became
standard models after independence. The area soon became a

testing field: the locals copied and innovated, improvised and combined new and old ways in order to regulate elections but also to make them come about. From the very basic question of the representative equation regarding who were the members of the polity enabled to exercise the political right of voting and who could they vote, to the more procedural aspects of how, where, and when elections were implemented: all aspects were, from then on, open to debate and legislation. Meanwhile, elections happened, and they became a decisive instance in the political life of the new nations.

Despite the overall presence of elections in nineteenth-century Latin America, until recently scholars minimized their relevance in the face of other, presumably more effective means to reach and stay in power. Tainted by corruption and fraud, they were deemed inconsequential, as the political game took place elsewhere. The prevailing literature also underestimated the importance of the right to vote; by adopting the progressive model of expansion of the suffrage, inspired by the English case, it measured actual histories against that mold, usually to find them lacking. In the last three decades, scholars have revised these conventional approaches, not only for Latin America, and by formulating new questions and producing original research, they have thrown new light on the electoral history of the period. In what follows, I rely on this recent literature to address the question of the suffrage and the dynamics of elections in nineteenth-century Spanish America.

The Right of Suffrage

In a republican polity, the individuals entitled to vote never compose the totality of the population living within its territorial borders. The right to vote has always been limited. The criteria for establishing those limits have greatly varied

throughout the history of representative regimes, and the suffrage was a central topic of the theoretical and political debates
around citizenship and the implementation of popular sovereignty in eighteenth- and nineteenth-century Europe and
America. Various criteria were used to introduce difference
among individuals that formed the presumably unified field of
the people, and to determine who could or should vote. In the
first years after independence, the postrevolutionary elites of
Spanish America were familiar with the main examples in circulation: the Anglo-Saxon model of the citizen as property
owner; the *citoyen* of France, where—according to Pierre
Rosanvallon—the only distinction "allowed by the abstraction
of equality was that which pertains to the nature of the actual
juridical subjects (age, sex, etc.),"[3] and the Cádiz *vecino*, a traditional word that was adopted by the Spanish charter of 1812
in a new context of modern representation. These examples
influenced the first experiences with voting under the new regimes, but none of them was adopted tout court, as Spanish
Americans tried to find their own path to representative government. In the following decades, the initial legislation was
subject to successive modifications, but overall there was no
pattern of gradual or systematic expansion of the franchise, as
was often assumed by earlier literature on the suffrage.

Who were the "citizens" involved in representative government? The term itself was initially used rather loosely. In fact,
the recently coined notion of the abstract and universal individual, free and equal to the rest, often overlapped with others
based on more traditional ideas of the body politic that evoked
the institutions of colonial and even precolonial times. First
among them, the *vecino*, which was not just a relic from the
past, but a concept recovered by the Cádiz constitution to qualify the voters: it connoted the grounding of the individual in
the particular territorial and social conditions of a concrete

community. This notion showed different levels of persistence across the subcontinent, but in most places, it tended to meld with, be subsumed in, and eventually wither away in favor of the polysemic term "citizen."[4]

By the 1820s, the boundaries of political citizenship were at the core of the legislation passed to regulate the different aspects involved in representative government. Despite the diversity of cases, there was a striking similarity in the criteria applied to define the potential voters. The right of suffrage was widely extended among the male population; in most places, all free, nondependent, adult men were enfranchised. Exclusion was mainly associated to the lack of autonomy, a condition that was considered indispensable to ensure the freedom of choice on the part of the voter. Women and children were therefore automatically excluded; they were considered to be dependent upon their family men. Slaves were also ruled out everywhere, but not "Indians" and the free black, as no ethnic distinctions applied. Frequently, free dependent males (servants, *domésticos*, peons, single sons living with their fathers, soldiers, ordered priests) were also excluded on the same grounds.

Different formulas were employed to guarantee the voter was not only a free man but also an autonomous one. Rather loose requirements of property, income, employment, or trade were often introduced as proof of independence. Thus, in Chile, Peru, and Colombia, among others, voting legislation included a list of either/or conditions to be met by citizens, in attempts at demarcating the ideal borders of citizenship. For example, after the final victory against the Spanish Army, the Peruvian Constitution of 1823 granted voting rights to all Peruvian men—"Indians" included—married or over twenty-five years of age who were property owners *or* had a profession or trade *or* were employed in a "useful industry," and did not belong to the class of servants or journeymen. In Colombia, the constitution of 1821 established that voters, besides their age (married or over twenty-one years old), nationality (Colombian), and literacy requirements (suspended until 1840) had to meet one of the following criteria: own property (at least 100 pesos worth) or have a profession, trade, commercial activity, or "useful industry," with no dependence from others as journeymen or servants. In a strongly hierarchical society, where colonial stratification still carried force, these precisions were important not just because of those excluded, but more so because of all those included—the established limits allowed for the participation of workers such as artisans, peasants, and employees, among others. In other areas of Spanish America, the franchise was even wider; for instance, in many provinces of the River Plate (later Argentina), after 1821, all free men (nonslaves) were enfranchised, regardless of their capacity, income, property, or occupation.

In other places, such as Mexico, the key attribute was to show a *modo honesto de vivir*, to have a known residence and mode of living. Although the constitution of 1824 left it to the state legislatures to determine the requisites for voting, in most cases they observed similar criteria: the suffrage was granted to male heads of family, established residents of the community, and "vecinos" who could prove to their fellow neighbors their honorable and autonomous way of life.

In all cases, besides the lack of autonomy, regulations set up explicit exclusions, which were basically related to the establishment of moral and juridical boundaries to the body politic.[5] Convicted felons, debtors, and vagrants were banned, as were those who did not belong to the community—which in turn meant residence but in some cases also an "honest way of life." Even sustained drunkenness or bad behavior could become a cause for exclusion.

Despite these safeguards, actual citizens often proved quite different from the ideal of the rational and cultivated man cherished by the enlightened elites of the postrevolutionary era, who were concerned with this state of affairs. The main proposal put forth to solve this contradiction between expectations and reality was the spread of education, which was meant to shape citizens and to instill in them the virtues deemed necessary for a healthy republic. In several countries, literacy was included as a requirement in regulations regarding citizenship, but with deferral clauses, which kept postponing this requisite for decades on end.[6] Thus, for example, in the abovementioned Peruvian citizenship requirements of 1823, the franchise was limited to those who could read and write. The enforcement of that clause would have cut off a high proportion of the otherwise potential voters, but in this case, it was explicitly postponed until 1840, and again and again later on in the century. In Venezuela, the same requisite, established in 1830, was temporarily suspended; in Colombia, the constitutions of 1832 and 1843 introduced literacy requirements but postponed them until 1850; in Bolivia, in 1826, the requisite was also deferred for ten years, and similar measures were adopted in other countries. Proof of literacy, moreover, was often limited to being able to sign. In the following decades, projects to extend education to the mass of the people never quite materialized, but dissatisfaction with the existing men-cum-citizens rarely led to constrain the actual boundaries of the polity. Apparent exceptions are regulations passed in the 1820s and 1830s in Ecuador, Bolivia, Uruguay (for those registered after 1840), and Chile, where nevertheless waivers to the rule of literacy were frequent.

One such mechanism was related to armed citizenship. In some countries, those who served the republic as members of the militia and later the National Guard, or were veterans of the wars of independence, were granted the right to vote, regardless of other requirements. Soldiers who served in the standing armies, however, were another matter, and the prevailing trend was to ban them from the suffrage, as they were not considered to be autonomous (see chapter 3). These provisions resulted in an expansion of citizenship in the direction of the popular classes, where most militia came from.

The shared principles that had drawn the postrevolutionary leadership to introduce political equality and erase the corporate distinctions characteristic of the colonial order had also inspired this initial tendency toward an extended franchise. The intense popular mobilization produced during the wars of independence, furthermore, had convinced the political and intellectual elites of the need to channel participation within the new representative institutions; therefore, the normative frameworks devised to shape the polity all pointed to a wide definition of citizenship.

In the decades that followed the initial experiments in nation building, these relatively wide boundaries were often put into question on different grounds. Political instability became the rule in most areas, and renowned publicists blamed the ample suffrage and the unruly electoral practices for the difficulties in achieving a lasting political order. By the 1830s, legislators resolute on limiting voting resorted to the example of French *vote capacitaire* to introduce new requisites on the right of suffrage. Yet such measures, where passed, proved generally short-lived.[7] Therefore, the prevailing criterion for exclusion continued to be the lack of autonomy. When compared with many countries in Europe and some states of the United States of America, these definitions of citizenship adopted during the first half of the nineteenth century were, indeed, quite broad, and they would remain broad for most of the century.[8]

The return to a relatively wide franchise, its persistence and sometimes its expansion, had ideological grounds but also resulted from the way in which electoral practices had been shaped. Popular mobilization became a key feature in the competition for power among different political groups, and elections played a fundamental role in that dynamics.

After the midcentury, the sustained difficulties in establishing a lasting political order, together with the ascent of liberal groups to power in several countries, and the political echoes of the 1848 revolutionary spree in Europe favored the introduction of some novelties devised to curb instability without shrinking citizenship. Although autonomy continued to be the basic criterion for voting, it was applied in new ways. The fact that slavery had by then been abolished almost everywhere, contributed to contract the number of those excluded on the grounds of personal dependency.[9] Also age limits were lowered, in some countries down to eighteen, in others they were kept at twenty-one to twenty-two. Clauses that defined citizens in terms of their social or economic insertion were eliminated for good in the cases of Mexico (after 1857); Colombia (1853 to 1863; from 1863 to 1886 voting rights depended on state legislation); Paraguay (1870); Venezuela (1857–58); Ecuador (1861); and Guatemala (after 1879). The last two insisted, however, on the literacy requirements, and so did Uruguay, but at this time with no deferral clauses. In Peru, from 1860 to 1896, such requirements were included among the either/or clauses, while in Chile, after 1874, it was presumed that those who could read and write met the income and property requisites, which were altogether erased from the electoral laws passed from 1884 onward. Thus, literacy replaced economic self-sufficiency as an indicator of autonomy. The case of Argentina offers a rather different pattern, as the constitution of 1853 kept the same criteria predominant in the previous decades in most provinces, now applied on a national scale. Citizenship was granted to all adult males born in Argentina (or naturalized), regardless of their capacity, income, or property. Exclusions were only applied to men who were institutionally or physically dependent, like professional soldiers and the deaf, as well to those who had broken the law.

For several decades, therefore, the initial relatively ample franchise was confirmed and even expanded. In some countries, the literacy requisite now became the main barrier, establishing a normative limit to an otherwise widespread right of suffrage. Although primary education experienced relative growth, and in some cases, it was made obligatory, most of the population remained illiterate, particularly in the rural areas, a fact that presumably barred a large number of men from voting. In most cases, however, voting practices blurred those limits: the requirement was met simply by signing the name or it was altogether overlooked on a partisan basis by the authorities in charge of the polling stations.

The tendency toward inclusion was persistently and increasingly subject to criticism, not least because the electoral practices that developed under those rules proved hard to control, and encouraged would-be leaders to resort to the lower sectors of the population for electoral support. By the last quarter of the century, suffrage norms experienced new developments. Common trends are, however, harder to trace, and while countries like Argentina and Mexico that had been for decades functioning with male universal suffrage, continued in the same venue, others tried new roads to citizenship. To go back to Peru, in 1896, together with direct voting, literacy requisites were introduced effectively, a clause that in practice meant the exclusion of most of the indigenous population and peasants from the electorate, a condition that persisted well into the twentieth century. And in Colombia, in 1886, literacy and income requirements were reintroduced for national elections, while suffrage remained universal at the municipal and departmental levels.

If for most of our period the right to vote was quite extended by the standards of the times, the number of the eligible was, in turn, more limited. Candidates for representative positions often had to fulfill property and literacy requirements, which varied depending on the office itself, on the national or local legislation, and on the period. This inegalitarian imprint was in tune with what Bernard Manin has perceptively labeled the "principle of distinction," widely adopted at the time in the United States, England, and France. In his words: "Elected representatives, it was firmly believed, should rank higher than most of their constituents in wealth, talent, and virtue."[10] Along the century, however, there was a tendency, in those older republican regimes as well as in South America, toward lowering the requisites, thus expanding the universe of potential candidates.

The early selective bias was reinforced by the implementation of indirect systems of representation, which were adopted by most—but not all—of the young nations.[11] Rank-and-file citizens did not choose their representatives directly; they voted for a more reduced number of electors who, in turn, were in charge—again, directly or indirectly—of the final selection. During the first half of the century, elections in two and even three rounds were common, and in most cases, electors had to meet criteria of capacity and income or property not required for the rank-and-file voters.

These regulations contributed to shape an electoral realm with an ample base and a hierarchical structure in the intermediate levels. The system was expected to moderate the results of the presumably passionate vote of the many and, by facilitating the rational exchange of opinions among the few chosen electors, to allow for a wiser selection of representatives.[12] It was, however, highly controversial, and throughout the century, there was a tendency either to implement direct elections or to reduce the levels of the indirect. In some cases, such as Ecuador in the 1860s and Peru in the 1890s, direct voting came together with the restriction of the voting rights to the literate.[13] In others—like Mexico and Argentina, for example—these steps were not tied to the right of suffrage.

Electoral Organization

These normative boundaries established the basic parameters for elections. But there was still a long way to go in order to produce voting. In the case of the candidates, even within the terms of the law, there was no established method for the nomination. How to select candidates? Who would select them? Was competition possible or even desirable? As regards voters, the laws also left lots of room for uncertainty. Within the republican frameworks, contemporaries found various ways of meeting these challenges, and elections became a regular feature of the different Spanish American political regimes.

For most of the nineteenth century there was no formally established method for the definition of candidates for representative positions. In the aftermath of independence, a widely believed assumption prevailed: the representatives had to be the best men available to embody the common good. Like in other novel republics, elections were considered as a means to select such men among those defined as competent. It was expected that the notables of each place would emerge "naturally" as candidates or that these would come about as the result of rational deliberation presumably taking place at the intermediate levels of the electoral procedures—particularly where indirect elections were the rule. Yet these expectations soon proved mistaken. There was no automatic selection of the best men for the job, while in the case of indirect elections, deliberation in the electoral colleges seldom responded to the "rational" patterns presumed by the guiding principles of wise government. Rather, and contrary to those values, competition for power triggered open confrontation among groups that sought to impose their own candidates. In that sphere, therefore, postcolonial Spanish America found similar obstacles to those encountered in the United States during the early days of the republic.[14]

Those were the times that scholars have conventionally associated with a first stage of politics in modern republics, where deferential relationships prevailed, and the figure of the notable—individual of social and cultural prominence—played a key role in the representative procedures. A subsequent phase saw the introduction of a new institution, the political party, and from then on, the development of successive party systems extending well into the twentieth century. Recent studies critical of this somewhat teleological narrative portray a more complex picture, and argue that, for example in the United States, actual political forms of sociability and electoral association did not necessarily follow that clear-cut pattern. This discussion may well apply to Spanish America, where the trajectory of political organizations shows the overlapping of the traditional world of notability and the vigorous one of partisan groups, while the notion of "party" and the institutions associated with it changed greatly throughout the nineteenth century.

For most of that period, the figure of the "party" was controversial. According to the ideas on political representation that prevailed in the first decades after independence, the nation was understood as an indivisible unit, and elections as a means to select the best men to represent the people as a whole (rather than to represent any specific interest or sector of society). The term itself existed and circulated since the early revolutionary days, but was then used to identify different positions in parliamentary and other public debates, and eventually, those who came together to put them forward. These clusters were presumed flexible and short-lived, and their involvement in electoral competition was considered inappropriate. Starting around the midcentury, however, parties developed into more permanent networks loosely held together by personal ties and relationships of shared commitment with a particular cause (and usually a strong leadership), and were increasingly active in electoral matters. More formalized institutional setups, however, only started to develop in the 1870s, as we shall see below.[15] Until then, in the context of rather loose party ties, the formation of electoral "lodges," "clubs," and "societies" became the practical and efficient actual means of association for the purpose of promoting candidates and pursuing the so-called *trabajos electorales*.[16]

As a form of sociability, the political club had a long history before it was introduced in Latin America. Associated with the Anglo-Saxon political culture of the eighteenth century, it gained international notoriety during the French Revolution. Clubs proliferated in post-Restoration France, and the revolutionary movements of 1848 saw the foundation of numerous republican clubs throughout Europe. By that time, they also expanded in Latin America. Under that denomination or the more general of "electoral societies," they operated widely in Argentina, Chile, Colombia, Ecuador, Mexico, and Peru, among others. These were initially very informal networks, designed to act in a specific electoral conjuncture and then adjourn, so as not to violate the sacred principle of unity that presided over republican ideals of the polity. Soon, however, they became more established outfits, which put forward political proposals, selected and supported particular candidates, and led all the stages of the electoral works. In institutional terms, they sometimes functioned within the lax framework of an existing party, but they could also be autonomous or even become the embryo of a new party. Parties, in turn, could be home to several and even competing clubs.

The proliferation of these electoral societies did not end with the problems posed by the persisting unitary notion of national representation. The aspiration to represent the people as a whole and the need to organize as a part in order to win were the source of continuous symbolic and material tensions. In that context, every partisan association claimed to embody the best interests of the nation, a position that frequently led to rhetorical wars, whereby each group accused the other of "factionalism," of trying to divide the body politic by representing private interests instead of the public good, and therefore, of lacking legitimacy to represent "the people."[17]

The overarching concern for divisionism, furthermore, had inspired the initial tendency to adopt the system of "winner take all," whereby the list of candidates that obtained a simple majority in an election was granted all the seats in dispute. By excluding minority groups from having access to representative positions, this system was meant to keep in check any tendency that might put the unity of the body politic at risk. Yet at the same time, it left no place to losers who thus felt motivated to challenge the outcome and typically dismiss it as the result of unlawful practices of their allegedly despotic rivals.

This whole framework whereby the political "other" was stigmatized as illegitimate posed great difficulties to work out actual political antagonism through regular institutional channels, and opened the way to the use of violence. Whether in a rather contained and ritual form or as open armed confrontation, violence thus found a rightful place within the values and practices of these republics (see chapter 3).

By the last quarter of the century, these features that had prevailed for several decades were increasingly put into question, as part of a broader change in the conception of representation and of the relationship between society and politics. For years, different voices had advocated the legitimacy of representing particular groups or specific interests and opinions in the political realm, a position that was initially marginal and only came to prevail within the new context. Formally established parties then became the preferred channels of political and electoral association, as well as the favored means to produce candidacies. They developed into tightly organized institutions, with prescribed rules and mechanisms to join in, choose authorities, draft platforms and programs, select and put forward candidates for elective office, define and enforce party discipline, and so forth. Minority representation fitted in with this institutional development, and most Spanish American republics, in tune with similar developments elsewhere, replaced the "winner take all" system by some form of proportionality in the allocation of representative positions. Both in conceptual and in practical terms, therefore, the figure of the party came to prevail and was increasingly cherished as the proper way to do politics in the new era. It was not, however, a smooth transition, and the tension between the principle of unity and the value of plurality remained an ingrained feature of fin de siècle politics.

Electoral Practices

The introduction of elections as a regular means to choose representative governments was a radical novelty of the postindependence era. Even though electoral procedures of some sort had taken place in colonial times, most people were not familiar with the institution of voting, and it took time and organization to instill that habit among the population. The liberal and republican elites played a key role in that respect; they preached the principle of popular sovereignty and propagated the values and norms of the new regimes, while at the same time they devised the practical means to produce electors and elections.

After the initial experiments of the early postrevolutionary days, a similar basic pattern of electoral organization developed, a pattern with local variations that proved long-lived. The initiative was usually in the hands of the political leadership. The relative few who aspired to rule had to resort to the many in order to win elections, a required step in the road to power. To perform in the electoral field, it was necessary to attract and mobilize followers, a task that was not left to the spontaneous and individual initiative of potential voters but, rather, was assumed by the heads of the partisan groups involved. They set out to recruit supporters through different means; among them, a decisive mechanism was the creation of organized teams of men ready to cast their votes on polling days and also to participate in different instances of the electoral struggles that usually took place on such occasions. The deployment of "forces" on election days was crucial, and although electioneering involved also other actions, there was no chance of winning without the collective mobilization of voters.

The ample base of the suffrage provided the political bosses with potential human resources for the formation of these groups, which critics at the time labeled "electoral machines." In them, relationships among the different layers of the leadership, and between them and the rank-and-file followers, were cemented by multiple and complex links and exchanges.

Scholars have often applied the term "clientele" to describe the body of followers attached to a particular party boss through ties of deference and subordination that were previous to any political engagement, and could originate in family networks, social relations, or the remnant fabric of colonial institutions. In this sense, it carries negative undertones, as it has been associated with traditional politics that presumably hindered modern forms of electoral behavior. A once widespread version subsumed political clientelism to social dependence, a picture that presumed that the owners of the means of production also owned the votes of their workers, or that socially prominent men could dispose of the votes of their underlings. Recent works show, however, that social subordination did not necessarily translate into political following, and that even if social bonds could play a part in the construction of political allegiances, they were not the only, nor even the main means behind the creation and working of these groups. Also, scholars like Richard Warren and Peter Guardino, for Mexico, and James Sanders, for Colombia, argue that the term allows no place for the agency of subaltern groups who actively participated in nineteenth-century elections according to their own will and protocols. Despite these limitations, the word "clientele" also points to a very widespread feature of electoral forces that is worth recovering: the basically asymmetric relations established between the leaders and the rank and file, in groups that were devised to operate collectively and act efficiently at the voting scene.

Within this very basic pattern, electoral organizations show important variations according to time and place. Many questions have received only very limited answers, such as how did these networks actually function, what type of vertical as well as horizontal exchanges developed within, or what motivated men to join a political force of that sort, among others. In the early decades after independence, networks were more precarious and ephemeral than later on in the century; elections were a relatively novel practice, and mistrust of partisanship cast a cloud of suspicion upon any organization associated with specific candidacies. In that context, and particularly in the rural areas, previously existing social bonds could play a relatively significant role in forging electoral commitments. But also, webs of subordination and sociability articulated in the aftermath of the wars of independence nurtured the power of local military chiefs (caudillos) who also played the electoral game. In urban settings, other types of relationships prevailed already in the 1820s. In Mexico City, for example, Richard Warren has persuasively shown that Masonic lodges became key mechanisms in attracting and conducting voters in favor of specific candidates, while in Buenos Aires, Marcela Ternavasio points to links of patronage generated through public employment in the provincial administration as the decisive element in this regard.

The formation of electoral clubs and associations in the following decades formalized the practices related to the recruitment of followers as well as to the organization of voters. In exploring these practices for the Cauca region in Colombia during the 1850s, James Sanders argues that "while some of the politicians' activities might be considered clientelism, most seemed more like electioneering."[18] And he goes on to describe the different methods parties used to attract followers from the popular classes, which included material incentives like food, alcohol, and "other seductions," as well as promises and pledges, plus other persuasive discourses delivered in person and through the formal and informal press. These mechanisms as well as those used to appeal to other social sectors did not eliminate the need to create tightly organized groups to ensure their active involvement in elections. The act of voting was not a given for those who supported a candidate; rather, only a minority of them actually took part in the electoral combats typical of this period. These were not limited to polling days; they also included all the activity that took place before and after elections and required the display of militant groups ready to face the different aspects of the electoral competition. Words such as "combat" or "battle" were currently used, and they are a clear reference to the conflictive character of many an election, where the display of physical force and violence (mostly but not exclusively ritual) was recurrent. Quite frequently, success at the polls did not depend so much on producing one's own votes but rather on stopping the others from doing so. For the leadership, therefore, it was more important to ensure the faithful and efficient organization of the electoral "troops," than to expand their numbers. And although elites displayed a rich rhetoric on participation, citizenship, and the development of the public spirit, they seldom encouraged the systematic numerical expansion of actual voters.

In fact, for most of the century voters composed a minority of the population. Despite the extension of voting rights to a wide majority of adult males, the figures on electoral participation show a rather different picture. Information on this subject is sparse, and not entirely reliable, but the available data all point in the same direction: actual voters usually composed a relatively low percentage of the total population—often around 2 percent, nearly always below 5 percent—while among those qualified to vote, the turnout was usually below 50 percent of the potential voters.[19] Besides these very general, nonsystematic figures, the existing information points to three relevant additional facts: the number of voters could vary greatly from election to election—and reach higher or lower figures than the average; no gradual pattern of relative increase or decrease in the turnout is observed, and finally, voters generally came from a wide social spectrum, with a clear predominance of men belonging to the popular classes, both urban and rural. Thus, it was not large landowners or wealthy merchants who made the rank and file of the electorate, but rather a variegated combination of men of various occupations, which could include artisans, urban journeymen, petty merchants, students, public employees, peasants, and other rural laborers.

These men formed the core of the electoral forces, which were often hierarchical structures based upon a dense web of unequal exchanges between the bosses (of different levels) and a larger rank and file. Men (and occasionally women) from different social and ethnic backgrounds took part in those stratified networks, which also were the site for the construction of political traditions and leaderships. Manipulation, political patronage, control, and coercion always played an important part in this story, but also motivation, negotiation, and conflict. Material and symbolic rewards, plus a sense of belonging and the actual integration in webs of sociability. were particularly attractive to men of the laboring classes, who could also profit from the protection offered by the political bosses in the face of military levies, police harassment, and other abuses. Ideology and rituals also contributed to the forging of political identities, which could transcend the personal bonds between each militant and his superiors.

The leadership of these clusters, in turn, consisted of men who did not play politics at the very top, but rather, operated at the intermediate levels and in local settings—in towns, municipalities, rural districts—to capture and ensure a following. Generally, they came from professions and occupations that involved regular contact with or some sort of dominion over other men, such as militia commanders and army sergeants, police officers, master artisans, foremen and overseers in different trades, tavern keepers, priests, teachers, principals of indigenous villages, and the like. They presided over the rank and file and at the same time mediated between them and the politicians of higher level, often the candidates in need of votes.

Electoral forces differed greatly in their origin, scope, membership, organization, and forms of action. Also, they showed different levels of cohesion and continuity, as well as variable degrees of stratification. But almost always they were locally grounded, and although they could be articulated into larger, regional or national, political arrangements, they generally operated on a more reduced scale.

There are numerous examples of specific elections in different countries that show these forces in action and illuminate some of the more usual forms of organization. In the case of Chile, for example, Samuel Valenzuela has forcefully argued that during the 1830s and 1840s, elections were mainly won with the votes of men from the National Guard,[20] who mostly came from the ranks of the urban artisans and other workers. Under the authority of their commanders and lesser leaders, militia units were ideal participants in elections: they were organized groups composed by regular citizens, who could collectively take part as disciplined voters at the polls and make use of their armed skills in the violent displays that were typical on such occasions. In the case of Chile, this mechanism worked in favor of the party that was in charge of the national government, but in other cases, militias did not respond to the powers at the center but, rather, to regional and local political networks. In Argentina, they became a disputed resource in all elections, when partisan groups sought to place their men in commanding positions within the militia and National Guard regiments, as well as attract and incorporate those who were already in charge of such units.

Also in Argentina, studies of elections in different provinces show that public and quasi-public employment played a part in consolidating partisan electoral groups. Men employed in the railways, the post office, the customs, and other agencies, were often recruited by foremen and managers to join their respective networks. Control over government resources gave those already in power a great advantage over potential competitors, but quite often electoral strife pitted different sectors of the official party against each other, so that leaders struggled to set foot in those government agencies that could help them earn their own following. Other circuits were less tied to direct relations of subordination at work, or in the militia, the army, or the police. Locally placed strongmen operated in city neighborhoods creating a following ready to take part in elections, and in rural areas, justices of the peace and other influential figures acted in a similar way. In some places, like Cordoba and Buenos Aires, associations that were not explicitly political could become involved in electoral recruitment when partisan inclinations came to prevail among the institutional membership. In the second half of the nineteenth century, all these methods for the deployment of voters were part of a wider set of electoral actions coordinated by the electoral clubs.

These clubs were also central to elections in Peru, particularly during the 1870s. Carmen McEvoy and Ulrich Mücke have studied the national campaign of the Partido Civil, and pointed to the innovations of political practices introduced by this party in its way to power. The leadership sought new ways for obtaining the support and the vote of different sectors of Peruvian society. Competition at the polls shows, however, that besides the novelties, older methods persisted. In order to win, Mücke argues, the party had to appeal to the "respectable society," but it also had to integrate "people of action" coming from the urban lower class. It was this group that "really carried out the elections," and to attract such men, parties had "to win their loyalty with cash, gifts, and invitations to festivals," and although patron-client relationships were not enough, they were necessary to guarantee attendance on polling days.[21] McEvoy also underlines the use of traditional practices. She points to the role of brokers in recruiting followers through different means, most of which required money that they were continuously claiming from their partisan bosses. In contrast to the modernizing discourse of the Partido Civil, paternalism, patronage, and family ties all played a part in forging the relationships between bosses, brokers, and the rank and file within the same party.

In the variegated world of electoral groups, societies that claimed to represent the will of the artisans were a novelty around the midcentury in several of the larger cities, such as Bogotá, Lima, and Santiago de Chile, among others. In demographical terms, artisans had always been a relatively important socio-occupational sector of the urban population that claimed a distinctive place within the working classes. As members of the polity, in turn, individual artisans were enfranchised citizens who belonged to the potential voters and often participated in existing partisan and electoral networks. Their collective identification as political actors was, however, a new development of the 1840s and 1850s. In the aftermath of the European revolutions of 1848, the category acquired political valence in Spanish America, as it came to represent an ideal figure of a virtuous worker and a model republican citizen. In that context, actual artisans who embraced political activism came together with intellectuals and politicians who endorsed radical liberalism, in associations such as the Democratic Societies in Colombia and the Sociedad de la Igualdad in Santiago de Chile, among others. These associations of mixed membership talked in the name of artisans as a collective force and displayed a rhetoric rich in motives alluding to work and workers. They were very active in politics; they participated in elections and in the militia, took part in revolutions and other armed confrontations, published their own newspapers, and put forward their claims in the public sphere. In the electoral game, their tactics were in tune with the rest of the voting forces, that is, they organized their collective presence of their loyal militants at the polls.[22]

This short overview of some specific cases shows that the term "clientele" hardly accounts for the variety and density of electoral organizations. Almost everywhere, these were tightly structured groups of militants, previously recruited and summoned not only to cast their votes but also to take part in the usual skirmishes and violent clashes with the other forces in competition. Potential voters who joined the ranks of the militant enjoyed the material and symbolic compensations of belonging to a particular political network, and incentives ranged from the more immediate rewards of patronage to the inclusion in elaborate webs of ideological and political fraternity. So the question of how and why these men, the citizens who actually exercised their right to vote, participated in these groups has no single answer, and the term "clientele" alone does not help us make sense of these practices. The abovementioned examples show a variety of patterns in this regard, all of which point to the complexity of these networks where the basic inequality of their internal relationships did not preclude a thick web of exchanges and negotiations within their ranks.

Non-voters

If voters composed a minority of the population that was recruited into the electoral networks, what about the majority who did not vote? The constitutions and the legislation considered elections as the proper means to produce political representation. The people, however, not always showed up on election days. Why? Actually, the image of a people eager to exercise their voting rights—put forward in conventional history books—proves anachronistic for many nineteenth-century societies. The political leadership frequently complained about "the indifference" or "the lack of civic spirit" among the entitled citizens—while at the same time, they preferred the certainties of electoral machines to the risks of a numerous yet uncontrolled following. Quite often, however, the mounting of these machines was a means not only to control voting but also to make it happen.

In many cases, as we have seen, rank-and-file voters came largely from the popular classes, where the incentives for participation could make a difference. For those who belonged to the upper echelons of society, in turn, personal influence with and family or social ties to the politically powerful could make electoral individual involvement seem superfluous. Even members of the parties' high ranks frequently skipped voting, so that usually only a minority of the socially privileged showed up at the polls. For the rest, including for those who formed in the growing ranks of the middle sectors, voting was often associated with old-fashioned factional strife, which could become quite violent. Their usual refraining from voting did not, however, preclude their participation in electoral politics through other means, and even their showing up at the polls on exceptionally contested junctures.

Elections were not limited to the act of casting votes. From the first steps in the designation of candidates to the proclamation of the final results, the electoral process implicated a wide variety of actors and required a vast array of material and human resources. Within that context, public actions and displays often included many more people than those who voted.

The periodical press was a key player in the political arena and had a significant role in electoral campaigns (see chapter 4). A second very visible means of campaigning was through the mobilization of people to express support for the candidate or the party of their choice. The leadership convened the followers to party rallies, street demonstrations, and meetings held in theaters, plazas, and other public spaces, while spontaneous manifestations of partisanship were not exceptional. Local bosses offered banquets in private houses and clubs as well as popular barbecues and festive gatherings in country haciendas and villages. All these activities included not just enfranchised men but also many of those who could not vote, including dependent men, women, children, and nonnationals.

Candidates had to win the favor of "public opinion" (see chapter 4). They therefore appealed to the people at large and sought to shape an actual following ready to buy or read the partisan newspapers as well as to express their active support in public. In times of the electoral clubs, these were in charge of promoting most of the actions in favor of their nominees. Later in the century, formal parties took over that role. These actions ran parallel to those implemented to secure votes and generally targeted a different audience. Yet they were a key aspect of the electoral process, whose legitimation depended not just on the voting rituals but also, and especially, on the gestures of public approval.

Contesting Elections

During most of the nineteenth century, elections were hailed as the true expression of popular sovereignty, but actual electoral procedures were usually criticized for distorting the will of the people. This view was not limited to the Spanish American republics but was shared in most countries with representative governments. The fact that, until recently, it also prevailed among scholars of the period, frequently led them to consider elections as basically corrupt, entirely controlled from above, and therefore, completely devoid of any representative quality.

Yet historians are now pointing in a different direction. Elections were a decisive moment in the political life of Spanish America. As the main formal way to public office, they were held frequently at the local, regional, and national levels.[23] They involved a considerable number of people from different social sectors, who participated in various ways in the rituals and procedures leading to the selection of representatives. Most of the time, elections were competitive, and although those already in power had relative advantages in the game, opposition forces had their chances to participate and win. Electoral results, however, were not always accepted by the political players, who often questioned the procedures and, therefore, contested the legitimacy of the outcome.

The voting process was a key instance of the electoral mechanism, and as such it was the subject of public debate and changing regulations. Its various instances were under scrutiny, starting from the right of suffrage and then going through the successive steps that ended with the recount and validation of the votes casted. The law established who the potential voters were, but their confirmation as such was often a matter of dispute. In the early days, voters were accepted or rejected at the polling station by the authorities in charge, and only later, in most countries, civic registers were drafted in advance listing the names of those entitled to exercise their right. These lists were, of course, frequently contested. Another important moment was the selection of the polling authorities who had a decisive influence at the voting sites. In the face of recurrent denunciations regarding official manipulations of appointments and the partisan inclinations of those in charge, there was a widespread tendency to establish detailed regulations to ensure their neutrality. These measures notwithstanding, the role of polling officers remained a cause of complaint.

The high point on election days was the voting. Mostly, voting was a public act. This practice was associated with a responsible exercise of the right of suffrage, and found prestigious precedents in other republican contexts. So, although there was a lot of talk about the benefits of making the vote secret, public voting prevailed—with few exceptions. As we have seen, when there were competing forces at play, elections brought about the deployment of organized groups in a regular show of confrontation not void of violent rituals. The space around the voting tables was either taken over by one of the competing parties that then proceeded to exclude the others, or it became the scene of the struggle between the different "machines" that sought to control the procedures. The deployment of security forces (the army, the police, the militia) did not prevent confrontation, as these were usually partisan resources used to back one of the sides in the dispute.

That kind of display was always denounced by those defeated on the occasion: their leaders used the word "fraude" to label the outcome, and pointed to the corrupt nature of the victors—blamed for pursuing their private interests instead of seeking the public good. The same methods were used by all parties, however, and despite the mutual accusations, and the regulations introduced to moderate the forms of competition, these mechanisms remained the rule rather the exception. After the voting had finished, the counting of the ballots on the spot gave more opportunities for cheating and for disputing the figures obtained by each candidate. Finally, procedures to recount and validate the ballots followed; for days, and even months, the action moved to the institutions in charge of those operations—usually, but not always, the legislative bodies or the judiciary—whose decisions were final but not necessarily approved by all parties involved. From beginning to end, therefore, the voting process was opened to criticism, to charges of "corruption" and fraud, so that there were few occasions in which the proclaimed results were accepted as legitimate without complaint.

These reactions in the face of elections could have different consequences. Quite often, the whole protest did not go beyond the public expressions of the defeated and their allies condemning the winners. Legal actions, in turn, could lead to the revision of the elections and even to their annulment. Sometimes, however, the losers resorted to more drastic means to challenge electoral results, and launched armed resistance that could build up into proper *revoluciones*, as we shall see in the next chapter.

Taming Elections

Despite criticisms and oppositions, for several decades the electoral systems in force lived on, showing similar dynamics and patterns of organization. By the last third of the century, however, this picture started to change. Critical voices grew stronger as electoral struggles were blamed for the persistent political instability experienced in most of the region. Electoral competition not only encouraged a popular mobilization of sorts, it also included open confrontations that made electoral results uncertain and dependent on the capacity of action in the field. The means for that kind of action, furthermore, were usually in the hands of provincial or local bosses, who controlled electoral resources. At a time when the search for a strong state came together with the concentration of power at the center, an electoral system that relied on the muscle of regional caciques, caudillos, and the like, and on the mobilizing habits of the lower classes encountered increasing difficulties to survive. In social terms, moreover, the expansion of an urban population with weaker ties to the traditional order also undermined the established networks, and increased the pressure for more transparent electoral procedures. In view of these developments, most governments tried to tame the electoral process. In some countries, legislation was passed to limit voting; in others, there were attempts at controlling political freedoms and competition more tightly than before.

These changes did not go uncontested and, at the turn of the century, new ideas and demands spread across the region. Among them, transformations in the dominant notions of representation, and in the political languages that articulated that concept, opened a whole new way of thinking about elections. The issue of the diversity and plurality of opinions and interests gained political weight, while the party became the prescribed institution to represent them in the electoral arena. The introduction of minority representation helped to channel political antagonism within the institutional frameworks, thus contributing to defuse appeals to challenge electoral results through the use of force. Revolutions, in turn, were increasingly discredited as a regular legitimate means of political action. Although not all countries experienced these changes in the same way, and some of the former methods and habits persisted beyond the 1870s, by the end of the century electoral norms, institutions, and practices were increasingly different from those that had prevailed since independence.

References

Aguilar Rivera, José Antonio. 2010. "El veredicto del pueblo: El gobierno representativo y las elecciones en México, 1809–1846." In Aguilar Rivera, *Las elecciones y el gobierno representativo*.

Aguilar Rivera, José Antonio, ed. 2010. *Las elecciones y el gobierno representativo en México (1810–1910)*. México City: Fondo de Cultura Económica/CONCA/IFE/CONACYT.

Agulhon, Maurice, Bernardino Bravo Lira, et al. 1992. *Formas de sociabilidad en Chile, 1840–1940*. Santiago: Editorial Vivaria.

Alda Mejías, Sonia. 2002. *La participación indígena en la construcción de la república de Guatemala, s. XIX*. Madrid: Ediciones de la Universidad Autónoma de Madrid.

Aljovín de Losada, Cristóbal. 2005. "Sufragio y participación política: Perú, 1808–1896." In Aljovín de Losada and López, *Historia de las elecciones*.

Aljovín de Losada, Cristóbal, ed. 2014. *Partido*. Volume 2 of the *Diccionario político y social del mundo iberoamericano*, edited by Javier Fernández Sebastián. Madrid: Universidad del País Vasco/Iberconceptos/Centro de Estudios Políticos y Constitucionales.

Aljovín de Losada, Cristóbal, and Sinesio López, eds. 2005. *Historia de las elecciones en el Perú: Estudios sobre el gobierno representativo*. Lima: Instituto de Estudios Peruanos.

Alonso, Paula. 2000. *Between Revolution and the Ballot Box: The Origins of the Argentine Radical Party*. Cambridge: Cambridge University Press.

Andreucci, Franco. 1995. "La norma e la prassi: Le elezioni irregolari nell'Italia liberale (1861–1880)." *Passato e Presente* 13: 34.

Annino, Antonio. 1995. "Cádiz y la revolución territorial de los pueblos." In Annino, *Historia de las elecciones*.

———. 1999. "Ciudadanía *versus* gobernabilidad republicana en México: Los orígenes de un dilema." In Sabato, *Ciudadanía política*.

Annino, Antonio, ed. 1995. *Historia de las elecciones en Iberoamérica, siglo XIX: De la formación del espacio político nacional*. Buenos Aires: Fondo de Cultura Económica.

Arenas Grisales, Sandra Patricia. 2003. "Representación y sociabilidades políticas: Medellín, 1856–1885." *Estudios Políticos* 22 (January–June).

Ávila, Alfredo, and Alicia Salmerón, eds. 2012. *Partidos, facciones y otras calamidades: Debates y propuestas acerca de los partidos políticos en México, siglo XIX*. México City: Fondo de Cultura Económica/CONCA/IFE/CONACYT.

Ávila, Alfredo, and María Eugenia Vázquez Semadeni. 2012. "El orden republicano y el debate por los partidos, 1825–1828." In Ávila and Salmerón, *Partidos, facciones y otras calamidades*.

Ayala Mora, Enrique. 2011. *Ecuador del siglo XIX: Estado nacional, Ejército, Iglesia y Municipio*. Quito: Universidad Andina Simón Bolívar y Corporación Editora Nacional.

Barragán, Rossana. 2005. "Los elegidos: En torno a la representación territorial y la re-unión de los poderes en Bolivia entre 1825 y 1840." In Irurozqui, *La mirada esquiva*.

———. 2015. "Las normas y prácticas legales: Soberanía *de jure* del pueblo y elecciones." In *Bolivia, su historia: Los primeros cien años de la República*,

1825–1925, vol. 4, edited by Rossana Barragán and others. La Paz: Coordinadora de Historia.

Basadre, Jorge. 1980. *Elecciones y centralismo en el Perú: Apuntes para un esquema histórico*. Lima: Universidad del Pacífico.

Bonaudo, Marta. 1999. "De representantes y representados: Santa Fe finisecular (1883–1893)." In Sabato, *Ciudadanía política*.

———. 2016. "Logias y partidos en la circulación y difusión de la(s) cultura(s) política(s) liberal(es) (1830/50–1890)." In *América Latina: De la independencia a la crisis del liberalismo, 1810–1930*, edited by Nuria Tabanera and Marta Bonaudo. Madrid: Marcial Pons; Zaragoza: Prensas de la Universidad de Zaragoza.

Botana, Natalio. 1977. *El orden conservador*. Buenos Aires: Sudamericana.

Bragoni, Beatriz, and Eduardo Míguez, eds. 2010. *Un nuevo orden político: Provincias y Estado Nacional, 1852–1880*. Buenos Aires: Biblos.

Buriano Castro, Ana. 2013. "Ecuador 1868: La frustración de una transición; Coyuntura electoral y prácticas políticas." *Secuencia* 86 (May–August).

Buve, Raymond. 1997 "Between Ballots and Bullets: Long-Term Trends in Nineteenth-Century Mexican Political Culture." In *Citizens of the Pyramid: Essays on Mexican Political Culture*, edited by Will Pansters. Amsterdam: Thela.

Carmagnani, Marcello, and Alicia Hernández Chávez. 1999. "La ciudadanía orgánica mexicana, 1850–1910." In Sabato, *Ciudadanía política*.

Chambers, Sarah C. 1999. *From Subjects to Citizens: Honor, Gender, and Politics in Arequipa, Peru, 1780–1854*. University Park: Pennsylvania State University Press.

Chiaramonte, José Carlos. 1995. "Vieja y Nueva Representación: Los procesos electorales en Buenos Aires, 1810–1820." In Annino, *Historia de las elecciones*.

Chiaramonti, Gabriella. 1995. "Andes o Nación: La reforma electoral de 1896 en Perú." In Annino, *Historia de las elecciones*.

———. 2005a. *Ciudadanía y representación en el Perú (1806–1860): Los itinerarios de la soberanía*. Lima: Fondo Editorial UNMSM/SEPS/ONPE.

———. 2005b. "A propósito del debate Herrera-Gálvez de 1849: Breves reflexiones sobre el sufragio de los indios analfabetos." In Aljovín de Losada and López, *Historia de las elecciones*.

Cibotti, Ema. 1995. "Sufragio, prensa y opinión pública: Las elecciones municipales de 1883 en Buenos Aires." In Annino, *Historia de las elecciones*.

Clark, A. Kim, and Marc Becker. 2007. "Indigenous Peoples and State Formation in Modern Ecuador." In *Highland Indians and the State in Modern Ecuador*, edited by Clark and Becker. Pittsburgh: University of Pittsburgh Press.

Connaughton, Brian F., ed. 2003. *Poder y legitimidad en México en el siglo XIX: Instituciones y cultura política*. Mexico City: UAM/Porrúa.

Cucchi, Laura. 2015a. *Antagonismo, legitimidad y poder político en Córdoba, 1877–1880*. Bahía Blanca: Editorial de la Universidad Nacional del Sur.

———. 2015b. "Antagonismo, política y partidos en las provincias argentinas del siglo diecinueve: El caso de Córdoba a fines de los años setenta." *Illes i Imperis* 17, GRIMSE, Universitat Pompeu Fabra, Barcelona.

———. 2015c. "Reclutamiento y movilización electoral en Córdoba (Argentina): Experiencias políticas en la ciudad y la campaña (1877–1880)." *Revista Bicentenario*, vol. 13, no. 2, Centro de Estudios Bicentenario, Chile.

Deas, Malcom. 1993. "Algunas notas sobre la historia del caciquismo en Colombia." In *Revista de Occidente*, 127.

Delpar, Helen. 1971. "Aspects of Liberal Factionalism in Colombia, 1875–1885." *Hispanic American Historical Review* 51: 2.

Demélas-Bohy, Marie-Danielle. 2003. *La invención política: Bolivia, Ecuador, Perú en el siglo XIX.* Lima: IFEA/IEP.

Demélas-Bohy, M. D., and F. X. Guerra. 1996. "The Hispanic Revolutions: The Adoption of Modern Forms of Representation in Spain and America, 1808–1810." In Posada Carbó, *Elections before Democracy.*

Di Meglio, Gabriel. 2006 *¡Viva el bajo pueblo! La plebe urbana de Buenos Aires y la política entre la Revolución de Mayo y el rosismo.* Buenos Aires: Prometeo.

Dunkerley, James, ed. 2002. *Studies in the Formation of the Nation State in Latin America.* London: ILAS.

Dym, Jordana. 2006. *From Sovereign Villages to National States: City, State, and Federation in Central America, 1759–1839.* Albuquerque: University of New Mexico Press.

Escalante, Fernando. 1992. *Ciudadanos imaginarios.* Mexico City: El Colegio de México.

Etchechury, Mario, and Ignacio Zubizarreta, eds. 2015. "Repensando el faccionalismo decimonónico latinoamericano: Desafíos y perspectivas." Dossier in *Illes i imperis: Estudis d'historia de les societats en el món colonial y poscolonial*, 17.

Foote, Nicola, and René Harder Horst, eds. 2010. *Military Struggle and Identity Formation in Latin America: Race, Nation, and Community during the Liberal Period.* Gainesville: University Press of Florida.

Forment, Carlos. 2003. *Democracy in Latin America, 1760–1900.* Vol. 1, *Civic Selfhood and Public Life in Mexico and Peru.* Chicago: University of Chicago Press.

Fowler, Will. 2010. "Entre la legalidad y la legitimidad: Elecciones, pronunciamientos y la voluntad general de la nación, 1821–1857." In Aguilar Rivera, *Las elecciones y el gobierno representativo.*

Gamboa, César. 2005. "Los filtros electorales decimonónicos: Los órganos y los procedimientos electorales; Perú: 1822–1896." In Aljovín de Losada and López, *Historia de las elecciones.*

Gantús, Fausta, and Alicia Salmerón. 2016. *Contribución a un diálogo abierto: Cinco ensayos de historia electoral latinoamericana.* Mexico City: Instituto Mora.

García-Bryce, Iñigo L. 2004. *Crafting the Republic: Lima's Artisans and Nation Building in Peru, 1821–1879*. Albuquerque: University of New Mexico Press.

Garrigou, Alain. 1992. *Le vote et la vertu: Comment les Français sont devenus électeurs*. Paris: Presses de la Fondation Nationale des Sciences Politiques.

Gazmuri, Cristián. 1992. *El "48" chileno: Igualitarios, reformistas, radicales, masones y bomberos*. Santiago: Editorial Universitaria.

González Bernaldo de Quirós, Pilar. 1999a. *Civilité et politique aux origines de la nation Argentine: Les sociabilités a Buenos Aires, 1829–1862*. Paris: Publications de la Sorbonne.

———. 1999b. "Los clubes electorales durante la secesión del Estado de Buenos Aires (1852–1861): La articulación de dos lógicas de representación política en el seno de la esfera pública porteña." In Sabato, *Ciudadanía política*.

Grijalba, Agustín. 1998. *Elecciones y representación política*. Quito: Corporación Editora Nacional.

Guardino, Peter. 2003. "Postcolonialism as Self-Fulfilled Prophecy? Electoral Politics in Oaxaca, 1814–1828." In *After Spanish Rule: Postcolonial Predicaments of the Americas*, edited by Mark Thurner and Andrés Guerrero. Durham, NC: Duke University Press.

———. 2005. *The Time of Liberty: Popular Political Culture in Oaxaca, 1750–1850*. Durham, NC: Duke University Press.

Gueniffey, Patrice. 1993. "Le moment du vote: Les systemes électoraux de la période révolutionnaire." *Révue Française de Science Politique* 43 (1).

Guerra, François-Xavier. 1992. *Modernidad e independencias*. Madrid: Mapfre.

———. 1993. "Las metamorfosis de la representación en el siglo XIX." In *Democracias posibles: El desafío latinoamericano*, compiled by Georges Couffignal. Buenos Aires: Fondo de Cultura Económica.

———. 1994. "The Spanish-American Tradition of Representation and Its European Roots." *Journal of Latin American Studies* 26 (1).

Gutiérrez, Francisco. 1995. *Curso y discurso del movimiento plebeyo, 1849/1854*. Bogotá: El Ancora.

Halperin Donghi, Tulio. 1972. *Revolución y guerra: Formación de una elite dirigente en la Argentina criolla*. Buenos Aires: Siglo XXI.

———. 1980. *Proyecto y construcción de una nación (Argentina 1846–1880)*. Caracas: Biblioteca de Ayacucho.

———. 1985. *Reforma y disolución de los imperios ibéricos, 1750–1850*. Madrid: Alianza.

Helg, Aline. 2004. *Liberty and Equality in Caribbean Colombia, 1770–1835*. Chapel Hill: University of North Carolina Press.

Hernández-Chávez, Alicia. 1993. *La tradición republicana del buen gobierno*. Mexico City: Fideicomiso de Historia de las Américas de El Colegio de México/Fondo de Cultura Económica.

Hirsch, Leonardo. 2016. "La República Proporcional de Buenos Aires (1890–1898): La consagración de los partidos políticos en la Argentina." PhD thesis, University of Buenos Aires.

Hofstadter, Richard. 1970. *The Idea of a Party System: The Rise of Legitimate Opposition in the United States, 1780–1840.* Berkeley: University of California Press.

Irurozqui, Marta. 1999 "¡Que vienen los mazorqueros! Usos y abusos discursivos de la corrupción y la violencia en las elecciones bolivianas, 1888–1925." In Sabato, *Ciudadanía política.*

———. 2000. *"A bala, piedra y palo": La construcción de la ciudadanía política en Bolivia, 1826–1952.* Seville: Diputación de Sevilla.

———. 2003. "La escuela electoral: Comicios y disciplinamiento nacional en Bolivia, 1880–1925." *Anuario del Archivo y Biblioteca Nacionales de Bolivia,* vol. 2003.

———. 2004. *La ciudadanía en debate en América Latina: Discusiones historiográficas y una propuesta teórica sobre el valor público de la infracción electoral.* Lima: Instituto de Estudios Peruanos.

Irurozqui, Marta, ed. 2005. *La mirada esquiva: Reflexiones históricas sobre la interacción del estado y la ciudadanía en los Andes (Bolivia, Ecuador y Perú), siglo XIX.* Madrid: Consejo Superior de Investigaciones Científicas.

Irwin, Domingo, and Ingrid Micett. 2008. *Caudillos, militares y poder: Una historia del pretorianismo en Venezuela.* Caracas: Universidad Católica Andrés Bello.

Jacobsen, Nils, and Cristóbal Aljovín Losada, eds. 2005. *Political Culture in the Andes, 1750s–1950s.* Durham, NC: Duke University Press.

Johansson, Frédéric. 2012. "El imposible pluralismo político: Del exclusivismo y otros vicios de los partidos políticos en el México de la Reforma." In Ávila y Salmerón, *Partidos, facciones y otras calamidades.*

Joignant, Alfredo. 2002. "Un sanctuaire electoral: Le bureau de vote et l'invention du citoyen-électeur au Chile á la fin du XIXe siècle." *Genèses* 49.

Keyssar, Alex. 2000. *The Right to Vote: The Contested History of Democracy in the United States.* New York: Basic Books.

Loayza, Alex. 2005. "El Club Progresista y la coyuntura electoral de 1849–1851." In Aljovín de Losada and López, *Historia de las elecciones.*

Loayza, Julio César. 2005. "Elecciones y participación política: El proceso electoral de 1876." In Aljovín de Losada and López, *Historia de las elecciones.*

Maiguashca, Juan. 1996. "The Electoral Reforms of 1861 in Ecuador and the Rise of a New Political Order." In Posada Carbó, *Elections before Democracy.*

Malamud, Carlos, comp. 1995. *Partidos políticos y elecciones en América Latina y la Península Ibérica, 1830–1930,* Madrid: Instituto Universitario Ortega y Gasset.

Malamud, Carlos, ed. 2000. *Legitimidad, representación y alternancia en España y América Latina: Las reformas electorales, 1880–1930.* Mexico City: Fideicomiso Historia de las Américas de El Colegio de México/Fondo de Cultura Económica.

Mallon, Florencia. 1995. *Peasant and Nation: The Making of Postcolonial Mexico and Peru.* Berkeley: University of California Press.

Manin, Bernard. 1997. *The Principles of Representative Government.* Cambridge: Cambridge University Press.

McEvoy, Carmen. 1994. "Estampillas y votos: El rol del correo político en una campaña electoral decimonónica." *Histórica* 18 (1).

———. 1997. *La utopía republicana: Ideales y realidades en la formación de la cultura política peruana (1871-1919).* Lima: Pontificia Universidad Católica del Perú.

Meyer-Aurich, Jens. 2006. *Wahlen, Parlamente und Eliten Konflikte: Die Entstehung der ersten Politischen Parteien in Paraguay (1869-1904).* Stuttgart: Franz Steiner Verlag.

Monsalvo Mendoza, Edwin. 2005. "Entre leyes y votos: El derecho de sufragio en la Nueva Granada, 1821-1857." *Historia Caribe* 10 (Universidad del Atlántico, Barranquilla, Colombia).

Morelli, Federica. 2005. *Territorio o nación: Reforma y disolución del espacio imperial en Ecuador, 1765-1830.* Madrid: Centro de Estudios Políticos y Constitucionales.

Morgan, Edmund. 1988. *Inventing the People: The Rise of Popular Sovereignty in England and America.* New York: W. W. Norton.

Mücke, Ulrich. 2004. *Political Culture in Nineteenth-Century Peru: The Rise of the Partido Civil.* Pittsburgh: University of Pittsburgh Press.

———. 2005. "El congreso, las elecciones y la cultura política peruana antes de la guerra con Chile." In Irurozqui, *La mirada esquiva.*

Navajas, María José. 2014. "Las controversias por la reforma electoral: Argentina, 1873." *Estudios de Historia Moderna y Contemporánea de México* 48 (July–December).

Navas Blanco, Alberto. 1993. *Las elecciones presidenciales en Venezuela del siglo XIX: 1830-1854.* Caracas: Academia Nacional de la Historia.

Negretto, Gabriel, and José Antonio Aguilar Rivera. 2000. "Rethinking the Legacy of the Liberal State in Latin America: The Cases of Argentina (1853-1916) and Mexico (1857-1910)." *Journal of Latin American Studies* 32 (2).

Núñez, Francisco. 2005. "La participación electoral indígena bajo la Constitución de Cádiz (1812-1814)." In Aljovín de Losada and López, *Historia de las elecciones.*

O'Gorman, Frank. 1996. "The Culture of Elections in England: From the Glorious Revolution to the First World War, 1688-1914." In Posada Carbó, *Elections before Democracy.*

Palti, Elías. 1994. "Orden político y ciudadanía: Problemas y debates en el liberalismo argentino en el siglo XIX." *Estudios interdisciplinarios de América Latina y el Caribe* 5 (2).

———. 2007. *El tiempo de la política: El siglo XIX reconsiderado.* Buenos Aires: Siglo XXI.

Pani, Erika. 2012a. "Entre la espada y la pared: El partido conservador (1848-1853)." In Ávila and Salmerón, *Partidos, facciones y otras calamidades.*

———. 2012b. "¿La voz de la Nación? Los dilemas de la representación política;

México, 1808–1867." In *Mito y realidad de la cultura política latinoameri-cana: Debates en Iberoideas*, edited by Elías Palti. Buenos Aires: Prometeo.

Pani, Erika, ed. 2010. *Nación, Constitución y Reforma, 1821–1908*. Mexico City: Fondo de Cultura Económica.

Peart, Daniel, and Adam I. P. Smith, eds. 2015. *Practicing Democracy: Popular Politics in the United States from the Constitution to the Civil War*. Charlottesville: University of Virginia Press.

Peloso, Vincent. 1996. "Liberals, Electoral Reform, and the Popular Vote in Mid-Nineteenth-Century Peru." In Peloso and Tenembaum, *Liberals, Politics, and Power*.

Peloso, Vincent, and Barbara Tenembaum, eds. 1996. *Liberals, Politics, and Power: State Formation in Nineteenth-Century Latin America*. Athens: University of Georgia Press.

Pivel Devoto, Juan E. 1942. *Historia de los partidos políticos en el Uruguay*. Vols. 1 and 2. Montevideo: Claudio García.

Posada Carbó, Eduardo. 1994. "Elections and Civil Wars in Nineteenth-Century Colombia: The 1875 Presidential Campaign." *Journal of Latin America Studies* 26.

———. 1999. "Alternancia y república: Elecciones en la Nueva Granada y Venezuela, 1835–1837." In Sabato, *Ciudadanía política*.

———. 2000. "Electoral Juggling: A Comparative History of the Corruption of Suffrage in Latin America, 1830–1930." *Journal of Latin American Studies* 32 (3).

———. 2010. "Newspapers, Politics, and Elections in Colombia, 1830–1930." *Historical Journal* 53 (4).

Posada Carbó, Eduardo, ed. 1996. *Elections before Democracy: The History of Elections in Europe and Latin America*. London: Macmillan.

———. 1998. *In Search of a New Order: Essays on Politics and Society in Nineteenth-Century Latin America*. London: ILAS.

Ragas, José. 2005a. "La distorsión de la voluntad: Corrupción y sufragio en Perú (1849–1851)." In Irurozqui, *La mirada esquiva*.

———. 2005b. "Las urnas temibles: Elecciones, miedo y control en el Perú republicano (1810–1931)." In *El miedo en el Perú, ss. XVI a XX*, compiled by Claudia Rosas. Lima: Pontificia Universidad Católica del Perú.

Rojas, Rafael. 2010. *Las repúblicas de aire: Utopía y desencanto en la revolución de Hispanoamérica*. Buenos Aires: Taurus.

Romanelli, Raffaele. 1988. "Le regole del gioco: Note sull'impianto del sistema elettorale in Italia (1848–1895)." *Quaderni Storici*, n.s., 69.

Romero, Luis Alberto. 1997. *¿Qué hacer con los pobres? Elite y sectores populares en Santiago de Chile, 1840–1895*. Buenos Aires: Sudamericana.

Rosanvallon, Pierre. 1998. *Le peuple introuvable: Histoire de la répresentation démocratique en France*. Paris: Gallimard.

———. 1992. *Le sacré du citoyen: Histoire du suffrage universel en France*. Paris: Gallimard.

Ryan, Mary. 1997. *Civic Wars, Democracy, and Public Life in the American City during the Nineteenth Century.* Berkeley: University of California Press.

Sabato, Hilda. 1992. "Citizenship, Political Participation, and the Formation of the Public Sphere in Buenos Aires, 1850s–1880s." *Past and Present* 136.

———. 2001a. *The Many and the Few: Political Participation in Republican Buenos Aires.* Stanford, CA: Stanford University Press. Editions in Spanish: 1998 and 2004.

———. 2001b. "On Political Citizenship in Nineteenth-Century Latin America." *American Historical Review* 106 (4).

———. 2009. "Soberania popular, cidadania, e nação na América Hispânica: A experiência republicana no século XIX." *Almanack Braziliense*, no. 9.

———. 2014. "Los desafíos de la república: Notas sobre la política en la Argentina pos Caseros." *Estudios Sociales* 46.

Sabato, Hilda, ed. 1999. *Ciudadanía política y formación de las naciones: Perspectivas históricas de América Latina.* Mexico City: Fideicomiso de Historia de las Américas de El Colegio de México/Fondo de Cultura Económica.

Sabato, Hilda, Marcela Ternavasio, Luciano De Privitellio, and Ana Virginia Persello. 2011. *Historia de las elecciones en la Argentina, 1805–2011.* Buenos Aires. El Ateneo.

Safford, Frank. 1987. "Politics, Ideology, and Society," In *Spanish America after Independence c. 1820–c. 1870*, edited by Leslie Bethell. London: Cambridge University Press.

Sanders, James E. 2004. *Contentious Republicans: Popular Politics, Race, and Class in Nineteenth-Century Colombia.* Durham, NC: Duke University Press.

Sattar, Aleezé. 2007. "¿Indígena o ciudadano? Republican Laws and Highland Indian Communities in Ecuador, 1851–1875." In Clark and Becker, *Highland Indians.*

Schelchkov, Andrey. 2011. *La utopía social conservadora en Bolivia: El gobierno de Manuel Isidoro Belzú (1848–1855).* La Paz: Plural editores.

Sobrevilla Perea, Natalia. 2006. "The Enduring Power of Patronage in Peruvian Elections: Quispichanchis, 1860." *The Americas* 67 (1).

Teitelbaum, Vanesa E. 2008. *Entre el control y la movilización: Honor, trabajo y solidaridades artesanales en la ciudad de México a mediados del siglo XIX.* Mexico City: El Colegio de México.

Ternavasio, Marcela. 2002. *La revolución del voto: Política y elecciones en Buenos Aires, 1810–1852.* Buenos Aires: Siglo XXI.

———. 1995. "Nuevo régimen representativo y expansión de la frontera política: Las elecciones en el estado de Buenos Aires, 1820–1840." In Annino, *Historia de las elecciones.*

Thomson, Guy P. C., with David G. LaFrance. 1999. *Patriotism, Politics, and Popular Liberalism in Nineteenth-Century Mexico.* Wilmington, DE: SR Books.

Tusell, Javier, ed. 1991. *El sufragio universal.* Madrid: Marcial Pons.

Urdaneta García, Argenis Raúl. 2007. "Elecciones y democracia liberal (Período 1830–1858)." *Memoria política* 11.

Valenzuela, J. Samuel. 1985 *Democratización vía reforma: La expansión del sufragio en Chile*. Buenos Aires: Ediciones del IDES.

———. 1996. "Building Aspects of Democracy before Democracy: Electoral Practices in Nineteenth-Century Chile." In Posada Carbó, *Elections before Democracy*.

Walker, Charles F. 1999. *Smoldering Ashes: Cuzco and the Creation of Republican Peru, 1780–1840*. Durham, NC: Duke University Press.

Warren, Richard A. 2007. *Vagrants and Citizens: Politics and the Masses in Mexico City from Colony to Republic*. London: SR Books.

———. 2010. "Las elecciones decimonónicas en México: Una revisión historiográfica." In Aguilar Rivera, *Las elecciones y el gobierno representativo*.

Williams, Derek. 2007. "Administering the Otavalan Indian and Centralizing Governance in Ecuador, 1851–1875." In Clark and Becker, *Highland Indians*.

Wood, James A. 2011. *The Society of Equality: Popular Republicanism and Democracy in Santiago de Chile, 1818–1851*. Albuquerque: University of New Mexico Press.

Zimmermann, Eduardo. 2009. "Elections and the Origins of an Argentine Democratic Tradition, 1810–1880." Working Paper 365, Kellogg Institute, University of Notre Dame.

CHAPTER THREE

Citizens in Arms

THE ORIGINS OF the Spanish American republican experiment were associated with war. The Napoleonic invasion of Spain, the ensuing armed reaction in the Peninsula, and the successive wars in America, which lasted altogether for fourteen years and resulted in independence for most of the former colonies, are at the background of the shaping of the new polities. Those confrontations entailed a wide-ranging mobilization of people and resources and the deployment of different types of armies across the vast Spanish American territories. In the political context following independence, however, the existing military landscape did not remain unchallenged, and a topic dear to the republican tradition attained a prominent place in the public debates of the new era: how to defend the recently acquired freedom in the face of both internal and external threats.

This issue had been at the heart of republican ideological and political controversies since classical times. The conviction that only those who belonged to the polity, the citizens, should be in charge of the defense of the republic, and that leaving it in hands of professional soldiers—mercenaries—opened the door to corruption and tyranny goes back to antiquity, and was still invoked in eighteenth- and nineteenth-century Europe and the United States. Standing armies manned by professionals and militia consisting of free citizens represented two very different forms of understanding military force. The latter was considered to be best suited to republican values, yet in the face of the empirical demands of war and in the name of efficiency, authorities oftentimes resorted to professional armies as an alternative or a complement to citizen militia. And although there was a long-standing tension between the two systems, time and again governments settled for a combination of both.[1]

In matters of defense, the Spanish Americans turned to these republican legacies and experiences, and early on they introduced the right of citizens to bear arms for the protection of liberty, a key piece in the construction of the new polities. The institutional expression of armed citizenship was the militia. Yet in this regard, as well as in the issue of professional armies, the early political leaderships did not start from scratch. Rather, they had to cope with the de facto militarization that outlived the wars of independence, as well as with the traces of colonial institutions and practices that were still in operation. They were also very aware of the discussions and legislation on this matter in countries that functioned as republican references.

Legacies

In America, for centuries, the Spanish Crown had kept regular forces—*cuerpos veteranos* of professional soldiers—as well as a rather irregular militia system, manned by the *vecinos*, for local defense purposes. These military arrangements were extremely variable, and it was only by the second half of the eighteenth century that, in the context of the Bourbon reforms, Charles III introduced new regulations in order to enhance the efficiency of the imperial armed forces in the colonies. Due to the high costs involved in the upkeep of the *cuerpos veteranos*, however, militia were the main target of reform, and they were rearranged and reinforced to cover most of the territories. The success of these measures was uneven and, at the beginning of the nineteenth century, the situation varied greatly from place to place, with the larger cities—from Mexico to Buenos Aires—being the main locations of the so-called *milicias regladas* (regulated militia).

By then, war broke out and changed the political and military landscape completely. There was a massive mobilization of human and material resources to back the war efforts. In most places, professional armies experienced a substantial and sustained expansion as well as an increase of their political importance. Militia, in turn, lived on, while various kinds of so-called irregular forces made their appearance in the war scene, usually organized by local groups in order to take part in the conflicts.

In the aftermath of independence, the effects of such widespread militarization proved long lasting. Alejandro Rabinovich has coined the term *sociedad guerrera* to refer to the situation that prevailed then in the River Plate area where, he argues, "the state of war became permanent . . . the normal condition of social life." He draws a compelling picture of such a society, which—he claims—lasted for several decades, until the 1870s. Whether or not the term is applicable for so long and entirely adequate to other areas, it calls attention to a crucial dimension of Spanish American history in the first decades of the nineteenth century, the profound and lasting impact of the extensive military mobilization experienced in the 1810s and early 1820s. In what followed, "war seems to have been actively adopted and consciously encouraged by the revolutionary elites, with a very important popular support."[2]

In this context, military organization was a key aspect in the formation of the new polities. In tune with the republican values prevalent among the postrevolutionary leaderships, the first efforts in this regard pointed to the affirmation of the militia as the institution that materialized the principle of the citizen in arms. In fact, after the wars, the authorities that came to power in the different corners of Spanish America reactivated the militia and redefined this formerly colonial institution in connection with the new concepts of the body politic and the sovereign people. They followed the prestigious examples of the United States and revolutionary France. The defense of the republic was to be in charge of the citizens, who had the right and obligation to protect liberty and fight against despotism. In tune with these convictions, most governments sought to reduce the size and influence of the existing standing armies and favor the militia. Nevertheless, debates around the military forces were intense, and in the following decades, the prevailing arrangements combined both institutions in very unstable patterns.

Controversies around this issue started early on in the new polities. Thus, for example, in the Mexican Constitutional Congress of 1822, a passionate exchange took place between those who favored militia and the supporters of a strong standing army. Their arguments touched upon various matters, from the danger of an eventual invasion on the part of the Spaniards to the problems posed by fiscal restrictions, among others. They also reflected different opinions regarding armed citizenship, clearly illustrated in the opposite views put forward by deputies Carlos María Bustamante and Pedro Lanuza. In support of the militia, the former said, "Some people believe that only the professional soldier can repel with glory the foreign invader:

this is a misunderstanding that I must put right: the militia soldier is a man with powerful ties; he is a citizen, a father, a family man; he is a man who appreciates his dignity, more so when he is in view of the enemy, because he then assesses what he may win and lose." Lanuza, in turn, claimed militia were only good to "preserve order, guard prisoners in jail, escort a convict . . . or go after a petty thief." National defense should be in the hands of the professional army: "to defend a military post, prevent a landing, attack a battle line, observe discipline and master the art of war; that belongs to soldiers and only to soldiers."[3]

This Congress finally decided in favor of reducing the professional forces and building up the militia; it also introduced a change in name: instead of "national" they became "civic" militia, thus stressing the new values in circulation. This decision was never truly enforced; Emperor Agustín de Iturbide (May 1822 to March 1823) counted on the standing army for support and strove to concentrate military power in the hands of professionals. The militia, however, did not vanish from the scene, and after the fall of the emperor and the proclamation of the republic, in 1827 the national Congress passed new regulations that gave the militia a key role in defending both the nation as a whole and each one of the states from external enemies.

During the same decade of the 1820s, militia were organized and regulated in several other places, such as Chile, Peru, New Granada, and most of the states of the United Provinces (part of the former Viceroyalty of the River Plate) and of the Central American confederation, among others. Ecuador established them in 1830 after its separation from Colombia as an autonomous state, while in Costa Rica, in 1834, the existing militias were reorganized and, with no standing army, they became the sole military force in the country.

In the following decades, the situation varied greatly from place to place, and while in certain areas, militia practically disappeared for some time—only to come back to life again later—in others, they remained a key military resource throughout the century. In fact, there was a widespread endorsement of the principle of armed citizenship, materialized in this mostly locally based institution that, besides the generic term *milicias*, could also go under different names, such as *cuerpos cívicos*, *guardias cívicas*, and the later favorite *guardias nacionales*, among others. Standing armies, in turn, shared the scene almost everywhere, and despite intense political disputes over their military organization, by midcentury most countries had settled for this double-tiered system, not unlike the United States' "dual army tradition."[4]

Although these arrangements usually proved quite unstable, they persisted for decades, with militias and professional forces playing different and oftentimes competing roles both in military matters and in the political life of the Spanish American republics. Of the two, only the militias were understood, in normative terms, as the embodiment of the people in arms, the guardians of popular sovereignty, and therefore as safeguards of the republican polity. In some cases, they also became bulwarks of state or provincial autonomy. These legitimating values were not the only bases for the importance of the militia, and other, more practical matters also played a part in the perpetuation of the institution until the last decades of the nineteenth century.

An Army of Citizens

Throughout Spanish America, the militia that took shape after the demise of the colonial order followed comparable patterns of organization, and by midcentury, despite the strongly local nature of these forces, they showed striking similarities in their basic structure, functions, and forms of action.

By definition, the militia was basically formed by the citizens. In fact, and not unlike potential voters, conditions for recruitment were highly inclusive: in most cases, all free adult male nationals had to enroll. There were local exceptions and restrictions, but the prevailing regulations opened the way to the inclusion of large sectors of the male population. The close association between the citizen in arms and the citizen voter can be traced to both the Anglo-Saxon and the French traditions, but the former model of the citizen–property owner never took root in the new republics. There were few exceptions to this general rule. Thus, in the 1840s, the ideal of a militia integrated by men with some means, who could pay for their arms and uniforms, was put forward in Venezuela and Peru, but with only very limited success. In fact, property or literacy requirements were less frequently demanded than in the case of voters; moreover, as mentioned in chapter 2, in some cases, belonging to the militia opened the way to the right of suffrage, regardless of other conditions. Age, sex, place of residence, and nationality were the main conditions for enrollment, which was generally but not always mandatory. Other, more specific, limitations included the exemption of certain trades and professions whose members were deemed nonexpendable, like public employees, journeymen in times of harvest, teachers and doctors, among others.

Ethnic considerations were seldom included, but in some cases, indigenous people were subject to special regulations. Thus, when and where they were subject to some kind of special taxes (successors to the colonial *tributo*), they were usually exempted from military duties. Such was the case, for example, with the militia and army regulations passed in Ecuador in 1835, which were applied in the following decades until the abolition of that sort of taxation in 1857. At the time, peasants and artisans were strongly represented in these forces, while the formal exemption of *indígenas* did not prevent their individual or, more often, collective participation in areas densely populated by indigenous communities, like Otavalo and Ibarra. In Guatemala, in turn, the indigenous population was in some periods and areas formally excluded from service in the militia, but some groups became an important presence during the war of 1826 to 1829, and later on, in the armies under the control of the successful political and military leader, Rafael Caldera. In the case of Mexico, Guy Thomson has perceptively described the involvement of indigenous communities in the National Guard, and has convincingly argued that "Nahua and Zapotec National Guard companies from the Sierra de Puebla and the Sierra de Ixtlán contributed importantly to the triumph of the Liberals over Conservatives in the Three Years War (1857–1860), to the defeat of the European intervention, to the rise of Porfirio Díaz, to his consolidation in power, and to his eventual demise in 1911."[5]

Even when and where enrollment was mandatory, not all men served. Exemptions and exceptions abounded, as did the hiring of replacements—not always permitted. Almost everywhere, the great majority of the recruits came from the lower and working classes, both urban and rural. These were often coerced into enlisting, but they could also enter the service as part of their broader political commitments. In the words of the Mexican liberal leader José María Luis Mora, "en ellas entraron las personas menos apreciables por su educación y principios."[6] This picture is rather incomplete, as the militia included other types as well, and not all those who had the required resources or connections to avoid it actually escaped their duty. Young well-to-do men with political aspirations were attracted by a prestigious republican institution, which was both a useful platform for building partisan networks and a crucial road of access to military resources. Also, politically minded men from the urban and rural middling sectors sometimes joined the ranks, and often ended up in commanding positions of different sorts.

Recruitment took place at the local level. Men were nominally incorporated to the regiment in their place of residence; they had to take part in regular training exercises and eventually go into effective service—usually remunerated. Militia duty was supposed to remain limited in time and restricted geographically, except during emergencies (wars, for example), when troops could be taken far away from their places of origin and kept for longer periods in the field.

In the early days after independence, militia companies were organized according to the colonial criteria based on social and ethnic categories, but soon afterward, those divisions were left behind in favor of a more egalitarian model based on the place of residence. Companies included all men within their area of coverage. This pattern was in tune with the new republican values that sought to erase the Old Regime sociopolitical order and claimed political equality for all citizens. At the same time, residence patterns usually entailed social and ethnic affinities among dwellers of the same district, like in the case of urban popular neighborhoods and indigenous villages, so that militia units often reproduced such uniformity.

Presumably, all members of the militia were equals, free citizens only temporarily subject to relations of subordination. In fact, however, the institution was strongly hierarchical, both at the overall level of command and within each regimental unit. The egalitarian principles prevailed on paper, and regulations often prescribed the election of commanders by the rank-and-file members of a company. This provision was quite important, for example, in the case of indigenous communities in

Mexico, where that choice was done in accordance with local traditions and practices, as well as in some areas with strong local leaderships. In other cases, however, this procedure was overlooked, nonexistent, or only applied to the lower echelons of the noncommissioned officers, so that superior officers were appointed from above—by the political or military authorities. In this regard, a widespread image associates militia commanders with large landowners, hacendados, or other socially powerful men who led their retinue (mainly workers linked by ties of patronage to their bosses) organized as militia units ready to play the military game, particularly in the rural areas. This picture may apply to some specific cases, but it is hardly valid to portray the prevailing complex nature of the militia organization of command.

Like the electoral networks, militia constituted hierarchical organizations with a broad base held together by vertical links of obedience and loyalty to chiefs and commanders, as well as by horizontal bonds of male comradeship and esprit de corps among their members. At the regiment level, commanders were key figures in defining and keeping these internal hierarchies as well as in weaving the connections with the larger military and political networks. They could come from different walks of life, but generally, the possession of some amount of political and social capital was a necessary asset, and different partisan groups competed to fill in the higher posts with their candidates. Military experience also counted. In fact, ascent by merit within the militia was also possible, even for men coming from lower social ranks. The main attribute, however, was the connection to local or regional networks of political power, where these forces had their roots and their main field of action. The chain of command could go all the way up to the president of the republic—as chief commander of all the armed forces—but more often than not the actual control of the militia was in the hands of municipal and provincial authorities. Commanders, therefore, stemmed from those webs of power.

An Army for the States

The militia was born as a colonial parochial body, and despite the institutional transformations introduced in the republican era, it remained deeply rooted in the local or regional political conditions. Its forces responded to regional leaders, governors, and *comandantes*, which operated with a great degree of autonomy vis-à-vis the central government. This situation was not just the result of political practices; it was firmly grounded in ideas and principles related to the quest for a decentralized state pattern. Therefore, attempts at shifting the control of these military resources in favor of a centralized authority usually failed, with few exceptions. Even when and where *milicias* became the Guardia Nacional, a presumably nationalized institution, it did not easily relinquish its former autonomy. In many cases, this army of citizens designed to defend freedom in the face of any tyrant also became an army of the states that protected their autonomy from the despotism that could be exerted by national authorities.

Thus, for example, in Mexico, the militia came to stand as a pillar of federalism. In accordance with the Constitution of 1824, the regulations of 1827 established the militia as the military force of the states, so that each state had to define its organization and functions. Before 1830, Jalisco, Michoacán, Oaxaca, Puebla, San Luis Potosí, Veracruz, Yucatán, Zacatecas, and the state of Mexico, all had their own militia. This arrangement was soon challenged by those in favor of the consolidation of a central authority, and during the 1830s and early 1840s these forces were alternatively reduced, partially dissolved, recreated once again, and so on, in successive attempts at diminishing or increasing the military power of the states. The invasion of United States' forces in 1846 led to the organization of the National Guard with uneven results in the different states, and in the following decade, the situation was again very volatile, with new legislation for and against these forces, and heated public debates on those matters. While centralizing conservatives favored the standing army, the liberals stood for locally organized militia. Many states struggled to keep these active, and after the Ayutla revolution (1854–55) and the War of Reform (1857–61), the successful liberals reorganized the armed forces, reduced the standing army, and expanded and regularized the National Guard as a state-based citizen army. This arrangement proved rather fragile during the French invasion (1862–67) and was once more adjusted to enhance the role of the professionals, under a national central command. By 1884, the government of Porfirio Díaz, who had commanded the National Guard of his own state and had profited from this position to fight and win the revolution that led him to the presidency in 1877, subordinated the institution to his now favorite military force, the standing army.

At the other end of the subcontinent, in the territories of the former Viceroyalty of the River Plate, between the 1820s and the early 1850s, each of the different provinces—held together as a confederation—had their own military setup, which usually included a militia and sometimes also professional forces. The constitution of 1853 gave shape to a federal Argentine republic and devised a national defense system that included a standing army and a National Guard. Although the latter formally depended upon the former, and both were under the supreme command of the president, the provincial governments were in charge of organizing the Guard on a regular basis. In fact, governors and other local authorities usually controlled these forces, which were deeply rooted in the provincial political ground. The situation led to a sustained fragmentation of military power, and to passionate debates as well as recurrent conflicts on who had the right to summon, mobilize, and exercise effective dominion over these forces. Very much like in Mexico, in Argentina the provinces claimed that control over their own citizen armies was the guarantee against the despotic tendencies of the national government. Those who were in favor of consolidating a centralized state, in turn, demanded that the Guard be entirely subordinated to the federal authorities. This controversy was long-lived, and only by the last decades of the century, was the dual system gradually replaced by a more concentrated military arrangement.

Colombia is another good example of the militia as a pillar of regional, provincial, and local power, and there are several others.[7] In most countries, the formation of a national government was a contested proposition; the persistence of strong regional authorities and a widespread resistance to the centralized state model were behind many of the political conflicts of these decades. Federalism was the institutional response to these de facto situations, but even when such schemes were formally adopted to allow for the distribution of authority between the center and the different parts, disputes about their share of effective power were the rule. And in most of these disputes, the militia played a key symbolic and material role: they were a stronghold against despotism as well as an indispensable resource from which to engage in armed conflict.

In these matters, the United States was a leading case. The Constitution had opened the way to the establishment of a dual military system consisting of a small regular army controlled by the federal government and the militia maintained by the states. Controversies over the relative importance of both institutions were commonplace in the first decades after independence and a matter of recurrent strife between federalists on the one side and antifederalists, and later republicans, on the other. After the war of 1812, the existence of a professional army was no longer in question, but it remained relatively small until the Mexican war when Congress authorized the expansion of these regular forces, while voluntary and state militia played a subordinate role in the conflict. In the following decades, the states insisted on their need to keep their own, relatively autonomous militia, and it was these forces from the Southern states that formed the initial core of the Confederation army. Nothing remained the same after that terrible confrontation, and the federal government became stronger and more powerful, not least in military matters; although the dual system persisted, the terms of the equation had changed for good. Spanish Americans were well aware of these developments in the United States, and they resorted to different moments of that history to sustain their arguments both in favor of and against states' control over the militia, reinforcement of the standing army, or concentration of military power in the hands of the national government. That example was particularly pertinent to those republics that chose the federal system of organization, very much on the pattern of their northern neighbor, where the militia came to embody not just the principle of armed citizenship but also the right of the states to have their own military forces.

Fragmentation

The coexistence of two formal institutions, the standing army and the militia, led to the fragmentation of military power. This situation was not only the consequence of the failure to unite them under a single command; it was the result of a combination of ideas, norms, and practices regarding the use of force and the defense of the polity that nurtured that coexistence and reproduced the unstable arrangements that prevailed for decades. Disputes erupted between those who insisted on the role of a decentralized militia in the polity and on the benefits of a fragmented military power and those who strove to strengthen a unified standing army and ensure its supremacy. Even though the existing professional armies also showed signs of internal divisions, collusion with local interests, and tendencies to insubordination, their advocates considered them to be more adequate than decentralized militia to secure the monopoly of violence in the hands of a single authority.[8] In that direction, they pushed forward for a systematic improvement of the army in terms of its discipline, hierarchical structure, and technical equipment, and for the subordination of militia to a unified, central command. The controversy lasted for decades, and it overlapped with other issues regarding the shape and features of the state in the republics.

In that context, the most frequent scenario was one of competition and hostility between professional and citizens' armies. There were various sources of friction, besides the already mentioned fact that they stemmed from distinctive traditions and responded to different ways of understanding the use of force in the polity. They also differed in their main functions, at least on paper. The existence of rules that prescribed the relationships between the two institutions did not suffice to guarantee a smooth partnership or a regulated subordination. The militia was usually defined as an auxiliary force whose movements and actions were restricted to a relatively limited geographical area. Only under special circumstances could it be moved to more distant locations and assume extra duties that were not too different from those of the standing army. In practice, these limitations were often overlooked, so that there are numerous examples of disputes between them regarding their respective duties and jurisdictions.

Tensions also resulted from the practical and symbolic distinctions between soldiers of the regular army and militiamen. Soldiers were associated with the figure of the "mercenary," while militiamen carried the aura of the citizen. Socially, furthermore, the former were considered to be either too poor to earn a living otherwise or outlaws recruited by force. They also had different rights and obligations. Soldiers entered permanent service as subordinates in a tight organization where they had to obey orders and go wherever sent. Militia, in turn, were formed by citizens with the obligation to enroll, participate in periodical military training, and eventually serve and then just for short periods of time, in locations close to home. They frequently—though not always—had a say in the selection of their commanders. Finally, soldiers were often explicitly excluded from the right to vote, while militia were not.

These differences should not hide the many actual similarities and connections between the two. At the level of militia commanders, the situation varied greatly, as in some places standing army officers were excluded from their ranks, while in others, on the contrary, the highest levels were assigned to professionals, who could thus rotate from one force to the other. As for the rank and file, the militia, like the army, mainly recruited men from the popular classes. In the field, their rights were frequently ignored and they received similar punishments to those inflicted on soldiers. Even so, contemporaries insisted on making the distinction between the two. The violation of the principles upon which the militia was supposed to function was a matter of recurrent public denunciations. Furthermore, the rhetoric of the armed citizen played an important part in the political life of the republics, not just for the elites. And militias came to function as networks whose role went well beyond their specific military purpose.

The conflict-ridden coexistence of these institutions was further complicated by the existence of the so-called irregular forces, which shared the military scene in several places and for relatively extended periods. Many of these organizations, like the "guerrillas" in the Peruvian sierra or the *montoneras* in Argentina, among others, considered themselves to embody the principle of armed citizenship and acted in the name of their rights to defend freedom and combat despotism. In fact, they operated very much like the militia and often intervened in political struggles as allied forces to partisan groups of different sorts, not necessarily "irregular," and in different combinations with formal professional and citizens' armies. In Argentina, for example, the leaders of these *montoneras* were usually former militia or National Guard commanders, who organized their men following that same pattern and acted in the name of their rights to the use of force. It was their enemies who labeled them as "irregulars" to question their claim to legitimacy. In the case of Peru, Cecilia Méndez has shown that "guerrillas" in the sierras "consisted of irregular armies of civilians, usually organized by their local authorities, which operated as auxiliary forces to the regular army"[9]—very much like militia in other areas.

These formal distinctions among the different types of military forces fail to account for the actual, rather messy coexistence, of armies that often did not quite qualify in any of the prescribed categories but "constituted . . . a continuum of war [military] practices," with no clear-cut lines of separation.[10]

Patriotic Liturgy

The militia was a vital part of the military system of the Spanish American nations-in-the-making and shared with the standing army the responsibility for their defense, both from internal and external enemies. Yet, as the embodiment of the citizens in arms, the institution had other important functions in the political life of these republics. Its role was particularly visible in three dimensions thereof: civic and patriotic liturgy, party politics and electoral practices, and revolutions.

Armed citizenship was a standard topic of republican rhetoric and symbolism. Militias materialized this principle, and therefore they were often hailed for their patriotism and civic virtues. Their companies participated regularly in public ceremonies and patriotic rituals, and the authorities praised them as guardians of freedom and representatives of the best republican values. Examples abound. Guy Thomson has perceptively shown the role played between the 1840s and 1880 by the National Guard of an indigenous community in the Mexican Sierra del Norte de Puebla on such ceremonial occasions. He also described the many connections the militia established with other organizations, like the *juntas patrióticas* and the musical *cuerpos filarmónicos*, in the collective celebrations of national and local festivities. These practices were deeply enmeshed in community customs recovered in the new context. Also in Mexico, according to Pedro Santoni, after the war with the United States, the federal government decided in 1848 to honor the so-called polko battalions of the National Guard for their brave performance during that conflict, and made this commemoration the center of patriotic rituals for many years to come.

In a very different setting, that of Chile in the 1830s, a new political regime introduced important modifications in the military organization of the country, and the National Guard, renamed Guardia Cívica became—in the words of James Wood—"one of the lead actors in the symbolic representation of order put on display by the new regime during national holidays."[11] On September 17, 1830, the guards participated in the celebration of Independence Day with a military parade, and the following year, the event culminated in a reenactment of a decisive battle against the Spanish, a patriotic ritual that was from then on repeated on the same date as a regular feature of those festivities. Government officials and military commanders did not spare words to honor the guards as bulwarks of liberty and order.

Similar displays of rhetoric may be found in most places in Spanish America. Thus, for example, in 1854 the governor of the Cartagena province in Colombia addressed the National Guard with the following words:

> Armed citizens! I salute you in the name of the province of Cartagena, as the loyal representatives of its valor and patriotism. . . . You have offered and spontaneously provided [your help], just like the sons of Athens, Sparta and Rome did in past heroic times. . . . Armed citizens! Let this be your war cry: Long live the Constitution! Long live the Republic![12]

And in Argentina, this type of speech as well as the parading of militia and national guards on patriotic festivities and civic occasions was a recurrent feature throughout the country and during most of the century.

Such lofty words of praise could easily change into sour accusations when militia contingents contested the current authorities or their superior officers and participated in rebellious actions against them. Also, when whole groups used their military empowerment to question the existing social and political order, like during the Caste War in the Huasteca, so well explored by Michael Ducey, among others. Quite often, even when the official language courted the institution, other voices of alarm expressed doubts regarding the virtuous nature of the citizens in arms. Thus, for example, at the same time that in the 1830s, after the armed conflicts of the previous decade, the Chilean regime strove to turn the Civic Guard into a symbol of order and union, critics mistrusted the citizens in arms, who could, they argued, easily engage in disorderly practices. Also, the fact that the government resorted to the guards as a voting force elicited negative reactions from groups outside the official party. On many other occasions, in different places, the partisan engagement of militia and, even more, the active participation of these men in rebellions and revolutions, triggered intense debates on their nature and their potential virtues and vices.

Electoral Engagement

On June 4, 1836, in Santiago de Chile, the opposition newspaper *El Barómetro* denounced the "emptiness" of popular suffrage during the electoral campaign for the reelection of President Prieto, and added: "A sad and embarrassing example of this truth is the custom that one observes in our towns . . . of bringing together at the time of a vote all the civic corps and veteran officers in order to distribute printed lists of candidates to them."[13] Three decades later, in the Argentine province of Tucumán, legislators of the opposition Club Sarmiento accused the government of "calling each one of the 'jefes' and commanders of the provincial National Guard to work for the candidature of Elizalde [the official favorite] under the threat of destitution of their respective posts."[14] These are just two examples of a very widespread practice: the active involvement of the militia and the National Guard in elections, and more generally, in partisan politics.

By definition, the citizens of these republics enjoyed two basic political rights, the suffrage and the right to bear arms, which for the most part were broadly extended among the male population. There was, therefore, a basic normative connection between voters and militiamen. In practice, moreover, although participation in the militia probably involved more people than voting, both attracted basically the same kind of people, with a strong representation of men belonging to the popular classes who were thus included in local political and partisan networks.

The militia convened citizens and assembled them according to the organizational and hierarchical criteria of the force. This structure could be productively put to use for purposes beyond their specific military duties, not least among them those related to electoral practices. While professional soldiers were often legally banned from the vote, these citizens in arms, on the contrary, often kept their rights even while on duty. Thus, the men participated collectively as disciplined voters at the polls, and they could make use of their armed skills in the violent displays that were typical on such occasions. Their sheer presence put pressure on the potential voters; it was also a dissuading factor for those who could not compete with militiamen in their use of force. Militia commanders and officers, who were themselves usually connected to partisan groups, operated inside the force to "produce" votes and to impose their men in the field. Such actions surely included coercion from the top, but there are many examples of a more multifaceted relationship between leaders and the following, whereby the militarized space of the militia was part of larger partisan networks whose rank-and-file members were not just unconditional subordinates.

The participation of these forces in elections did not necessarily mean support for the current official candidates. Militia and the National Guard were not strictly government forces. Deeply rooted in the local political world, their battalions could be in the opposition to candidacies supported by the central or "national" authorities, but also within the regional and local scenes, they could respond to different partisan groups in competition. The power to appoint commanders and organize the forces was a key instrument for the control of their electoral performance, and therefore, where governors had that right, they operated swiftly to ensure their own men were in charge. Yet this maneuvering did not guarantee the tight domination of every battalion, and because all partisan groups strove to gain influence upon them through sympathetic commanding officers, their electoral behavior could prove contrary to the interests of their official bosses.

Chile offers an interesting example of the electoral weight of a National Guard controlled from above. In 1830, the military and political success of the party that strove for the consolidation of a centralized authority favored the concentration of power in the hands of the national government. Among the important institutional reforms introduced by the new administration, under the leadership of Diego Portales, the reorganization of the military had decisive political consequences. The National Guard gained a privileged role in the regime; it was expanded and restructured to enforce order and discipline among the ranks, now firmly under the command of officers appointed by and loyal to the national authorities. It also became a means of exerting control over the members of the working classes, and artisans were a key presence in most battalions of the urban areas.

In those years, the Guard also became a fundamental player in the electoral game. In this case, the official candidates could count on the votes cast by these "citizens in arms" in the different parts of the country. The opposition complained, but the system proved efficient for those already in power—at least until the late 1840s. A first visible attempt at gaining the favor of the guards to compete against an official presidential candidate took place on the occasion of the elections of 1846. The followers of Ramón Freire put into circulation the newssheet

El Guardia Nacional to attract the attention of the rank-and-file citizens in arms, with meager results. The incumbent, Francisco Bulnes, was reelected by a large majority. On the day of the election, however, there were tumultuous protests in Valparaíso, a city where three years later the opposition candidate won the seat as representative in Congress against the name put forward by the government. Presumably, some guards had disobeyed their orders, a fact that led to increasing unease regarding the voting power of these men in arms who could eventually go their own way. In fact, in the years that followed, this tendency was further accentuated with the increasing mobilization of the liberal party, the rise of certain radical groups within it, and the creation of the Sociedad de la Igualdad, which put forward an egalitarian agenda that included a strong appeal to the workers, particularly the artisans—with limited success. The mobilization of opposition groups was intense but short-lived, and it went beyond the electoral disputes to tread the roads of armed insurrection, finally defeated by government forces with the participation of the National Guard. Nevertheless, concern about the potential for subordination within the institution prompted the authorities to better articulate it with an increasingly robust professional army.

In neighboring Argentina, after the constitution of the federal republic in 1853, the Guard was also a relevant electoral actor, but in a rather different direction from the Chilean case. At least until the 1880s, the recently created federal government did not control that force, which was basically managed by the provincial authorities. The governors named their own men to command the battalions and tried to make sure that they could count on them and their rank and file during elections. Between 1863 and 1877, enrollment in the National Guard was a requisite for voters, so that commanders could easily manipulate the granting of certificates in order to suit their partisan interests. Also, actual guards on duty could vote, and they also participated in the organization and control of the space around the polling stations. Not always, however, the current provincial authorities could effectively depend upon the Guard, whose battalions often changed sides, or joined the ranks of a partisan group that did not respond to the official candidates. The federal government also tried to influence the designation of commanders and to gain the favor of those already in charge, as well as to negotiate with the provincial administrations the control of the force. Throughout this period, therefore, the National Guard was a key political player, which did not respond to a single institutional or political authority; rather, its power both in military and partisan matters was fragmented. In each province, and sometimes in different areas within a province, it was enmeshed in the local networks of political action. Regional alliances were also frequent, but a unified command was almost out of the question. This situation exceeded the electoral game and reached its most stirring effects when the partisan strife led to armed confrontation and revolutions.

Revolutions

The deployment of armed resources was a regular feature of Spanish American politics. In the form of revolutions and *levantamientos* (uprisings) of various kinds, political actors resorted to military force to question, challenge, and eventually depose those in power. This was not an exceptional move; rather, it was an accepted way of political intervention.

Throughout the nineteenth century, most countries experienced frequent actions of this sort, successful and unsuccessful. In Mexico, for example, more than 1,500 *pronuncia-*

mientos were staged between 1821, when the Plan de Iguala proclaimed independence, and 1876, when the Plan de Tuxtepec opened the road to power for Porfirio Díaz. These were manifestos put forward to question, formulate demands to, and put pressure upon the authorities, and very often—though not always—culminated in a military action against them. In Argentina, at the other end of the subcontinent, a nineteenth-century observer counted 117 *levantamientos* between 1862 and 1868, and many more both national and local took place during the rest of the century. Chile, in turn, saw less of this type of actions, but all the same, four full-fledged armed interventions were launched to contest the national authorities in 1829–30, 1851, 1859, and 1891. And Colombia experienced on average a major war every seven years. The rest of the Spanish American republics have a similar record.[15]

The story has been told many times, from different viewpoints, and has led scholars and other observers to put forward various interpretations of such widespread use of force and display of armed resources in the political life of the region. Until recent years, most of them cast a condemning eye on these recurrent practices, considered to be the result of retrograde political habits and an obstacle in the road to modernization. In a pioneer critique to those perceptions included in an edited book published in 2000, Rebecca Earle called for a rejection of the prevailing accounts of the nineteenth century in Latin America as a "period of epic chaos," and on the basis of the essays included in the volume, proposed that "elections, *pronunciamientos* and revolt should perhaps be seen as part of the normal, if problematic, functioning of nineteenth century politics."[16] Since then, scholars have revisited this topic under new light and have tried to understand revolutions and other forms of armed confrontations in context.

Within the republican framework adopted by the Spanish American polities, the figure of the citizen-in-arms had a central place among the values and the institutions of self-government as it was adopted after independence. From then on and for most of the century, as we have seen, citizens—as guardians of popular sovereignty—had the right and the obligation to bear arms in defense of freedom and in the face of any abuses of power. The right to insurrection was grounded in the theory of natural rights—which was widely accepted at the time and had precedence over positive law—and it opened the way to challenge the existing authorities on the charge of alleged despotism and to the deployment of armed resources to back this challenge. In republican terms, acting against a despotic authority was a not only a right but also an obligation, a civic duty.

Spanish American revolutions were often grounded in that right. In tune with the use of the concept of revolution that was quite widespread at the time, revolutionaries called for the restoration of some lost liberties and demanded to return to an institutional order presumably infringed by a despotic government.[17] In this context, revolutions were not seen as a rupture. In the political road to power, where elections played a prominent legal role, the military mobilization of the people could follow, considered to be a legitimate step in a continuum of available political actions that could culminate in a *levantamiento*. Elections, moreover, were among the more frequent explicit motives behind such confrontations. Rebels denounced official manipulation and fraud to justify the use of force, which could also be grounded on other claims related to the exercise of government power and the need to defend rights and liberties.

The limits of what could count as legitimate were, however, always in dispute. Thus, armed revolts that put forward social demands and confronted the existing social system defied the established limits, and although their promoters could use the language of republican citizenship to express their claims, they actually challenged the accepted protocols of political revolutions.

The term *revolution*, in turn, experienced important variations throughout the century, but for most of the time, it had a positive connotation related to popular reaction against despotism or tyranny. Those who launched these actions usually claimed that their particular armed rebellion was, in fact, a revolution, while their enemies questioned that claim and used more negatively charged terms, such as *rebellion* or *insurrection* against the legitimate authorities. This positive connotation of the concept of *revolution* associated with the notion *resistance* to despotism did not always prevail, however, and in the last decades of the century it gained new meanings that implied radical change rather than the search for the "restoration" of lost liberties.

In any case, revolutions in different forms and under various names became a regular feature of Spanish American politics. The contrast in this regard with the United States—the main model for republican polity for nineteenth-century Latin Americans—is worth exploring.[18] The northern nation also witnessed rebellions that resorted to arguments not so different from the ones used by its neighbors to the south. The best-known examples are the Whiskey Rebellion of 1794, the Fries's Rebellion of 1800, the Baltimore Riot in 1812, the Dorr Rebellion of 1842, and the post–Civil War insurgencies in the Southern states. These few armed actions posing demands to the established powers did not generate large-scale revolts, they elicited strong disapproval from various quarters, and they were easily subdued. A different question arises, however, with the Civil War, which may itself be considered a case of internal rebellion, where—by the way—militia played a significant role, particularly in the formation of the Confederate army. This challenge escalated into a full-fledged civil war with no equivalent in the Spanish American republics. None of the revolutions in the south reached the scale—in terms of duration, geographical reach, and number of casualties—of that conflict, in a country that had previously known only a handful of such events. Thus, the highly coveted political stability reached in the United States after some initial fears was suddenly shattered by a conflict that evoked the volatile and strongly despised Spanish American "anarchy" and exposed the fragility of the republic's political order. The outcome of the war, and the measures taken by the Lincoln administration during the conflict, strengthened the federal government, and in the end, made any actions against it very hard to sustain. In fact, a wave of insurrections in the Southern states during Reconstruction "did not seek to overthrow the *federal government*. . . . Rather, their objective was to remove the Republican state governments . . . and replace them with Democratic ones."[19]

Not all revolutions in the Spanish American republics demanded the fall of the central government either, and although some of them acquired national scope, many more took place at the local and regional levels. In all cases, however, revolutions involved political actors who resorted to military means in order to dispute their claims, and were ready to fight their opponents not just in elections but also through the use of force. Most of these events were preceded by a public declaration of some sort, which stated the causes that had led their leaders to action, and proposed a plan for the future. Thus, for example, in Mexico, from the failed localized revolt of San Luis Potosí in 1837 to the very successful uprising headed by Porfirio Díaz in Mexico in 1876, most of the armed confrontations of the century followed a *pronunciamiento*. On April 14, 1837, in the city of San Luis Potosí, under the title "Long live the Federation!" a group of "officers and citizens" proclaimed their opposition to the current government. The first point of their declaration stated that "the independence of the nation, which is the most sacred object of all Mexicans, finds itself threatened in different ways, and most particularly by our ancient rulers," and after enumerating the evidence to back that claim, the sixth and last point declared that: "For this reason the Mexican nation finds itself in a state of complete disarray as a result of the absence of laws that may safeguard individual guarantees and national liberties; and thus the undersigned hereby pronounce of the reestablishment of the federal system." That was, indeed, their main proclaimed objective, to restore the "popular federal system that was adopted freely and spontaneously by the nation in the year of 1824." Almost forty years later, the Plan de Tuxtepec, of January 10, 1876, was launched to protest the recent reelection of Sebastián Lerdo de Tejada to the presidency, and stated the main causes for the pronouncement: that the national government had abused the political system, "despising and violating norms and laws"; that suffrage had "become a farce"; that democracy was mocked, and the sovereignty of the states had been repeatedly infringed by the federal authorities, among others. Thus, "in the name of an insulted society and the vilified Mexican people, we raise the banner of war against our common oppressors."[20]

In Argentina, in turn, two examples from very different political actors may illustrate the shared terms of the *proclamas* that preceded revolutions. In this case, both ended up in failure: the rebellion, in 1863, of the *montoneras* in the northwest, against the central government then headed by Bartolomé Mitre, and the one headed by Mitre himself, in 1874, after losing an election that he claimed was rigged by the current authorities. In the first case, General Ángel Vicente Peñaloza,

"Chacho," summoned the people, and particularly the "Guardias Nacionales," to "combat . . . the evils that afflict our *patria* and repel with noble efforts its oppressing tyrants" and "to reconquer our sacred rights and liberties." Mitre, in turn, issued in 1874 a manifesto when the revolution was already in motion. He explained that, no matter how hard he had tried to avoid resorting to arms, the systematic exercise of fraud to bend the result of the elections had left him no choice. The revolution was the only possible way to reclaim the usurped rights and the suppressed public liberties. In fact, he wrote, "the revolution was a right and a necessity and not to carry it through . . . would amount to a dishonor that would prove that we were incapable and unworthy of keeping and deserving the lost liberties."[21]

The basic arguments were, as illustrated by these examples—only a few among many more—very similar, and all of them pointed to the inevitability of resorting to arms when the authorities violated the people's public liberties and rights. It was the honorable thing to do. The use of force in regular politics was deeply enmeshed in an intricate web of norms and practices whose contours responded to widely accepted, albeit variable, rules of the political game. In that context, armed confrontations took place as part of a competitive political life driven by struggles for power and by disagreements over the territorial and institutional shaping of the republics. Political actors resorted to all recognized means available in order to dispute their claims—from elections to personal lobbying, the war of words through the press, the mobilization of followers in public demonstrations of various sorts, and so on—and they were ready to fight their opponents also through the use of force—a move that was not necessarily considered illegitimate. At the same time, if resorting to violence could count as legitimate, the outcome of an armed confrontation did not suffice to grant legitimacy to the victors, and these had to validate their titles at the polls, as well as in the realm of "public opinion." Thus, revolutions were embedded in republican politics and belonged to the usual repertoire of most political players.

The armed option required military resources, both technical and human. The fragmentation of military forces—particularly the double-tiered arrangement of a standing army and militia with deep local roots—was at the heart of the system, and its persistence was strongly upheld by important figures of the ruling cadres as well as by wider sectors of the population. Most political networks included some connection with and control of armed resources. The militia fitted well within this framework. In normative terms, they represented the people in arms. In practice, these forces were locally based; they responded to regional caudillos, provincial governors, and local commanders, and were scarcely controlled by the central governments. Therefore, revolutionaries usually made use of such resources, which did not preclude their resorting also to the professional armies. Partisanship ran through both types of military institutions, so that these confrontations could easily pit different militia battalions or army regiments against each other. National authorities sought to subordinate the standing army—or at least to ensure its loyalty. But almost by definition the militia challenged all attempts at monopolizing military force at the center. By the last quarter of the century, this situation was vigorously addressed in most of the Spanish America nations: as part of the drive to strengthen state power, militia and National Guards were either eliminated or put under the tight control of increasingly centralized standing armies.

Until then, however, most uprisings involved both types of armies, plus the "irregular" forces that often joined in the struggles. They also recruited the cooperation of sectors of the population who were not enlisted, but participated in both material and symbolic collaboration with the rebels. Money was raised among sympathizers, friends in public office, and eventually, also by confiscating enemy property. Public demonstrations of support adopted different forms and tried to convey the popularity of the cause. In this regard, newspapers and other published materials played a crucial role by promoting, advertising, and seeking to legitimize the event. On the other side, the challenged authorities not only resorted to the military forces they could control but also tried to mobilize the population to question and censor the rebels' credentials. Despite the strong feelings seemingly put in motion by all these movements, and regardless of how much blood was spilled on and around the battlefields, later punishments of the defeated party were usually relatively mild; the victors were lenient with the troops, and the leadership could be penalized with exile, proscription, and sometimes prison, often shortened by periodic amnesties. The application of the death penalty was truly exceptional.

In short, revolutions were not just military undertakings; rather, they were a political move embedded in republican traditions and practices. They were, however, always considered out of the ordinary, not the normal development of institutional life but one that required explicit and convincing arguments to justify them. Criticism of such practices did not only stem from those challenged on each occasion but also from publicists who saw these events as the expression of anarchy, archaic political habits, the negative influence of caudillos and caciques, and as a deeply ingrained constraint to modernity. These views have profoundly influenced the later understanding of revolutions, so that for a long time, scholars have seen them under that light, overlooking the actual place they had in nineteenth-century republican politics.

Such interpretations are strongly influenced by a widespread vision of Latin America as a basically violent region of the world—both today and in the past. Within that framework, nineteenth-century revolutions are conventionally portrayed as the most obvious expressions of the collective violence that permeated the political life of the period. While in a modern polity the use of force is presumably eradicated from civil society and located exclusively in the realm of the state, the persistence of various forms of violence in the Spanish American republics appears as an archaic obstacle to the progressive road leading from a traditional to a modern society. Yet in those republics, as we have seen, political violence was not merely a relic from the past or an atavistic reaction against modernization. Although some expressions of collective action experienced in those decades of rapid social, economic, cultural, and political change may fit that picture, most of them did not. In fact, it was modernization itself that introduced new forms of political violence into the scene. Rather than casting a contemporary condemning eye on such forms and using "violence" as an essential and value-charged notion, therefore, this chapter has tried to disaggregate the concept and to understand specific violent practices in historical context. This context was always in flux, and by the end of the century, new perceptions and considerations on violence came together with changes in its prevailing forms of representation that were in tune with the broader political mood of the incoming era.

References

AA.VV. 2010. *La construcción de la Nación Argentina: El rol de las Fuerzas Armadas*. Buenos Aires: Ministerio de Defensa.

Aguilar Rivera, José Antonio, and Rafael Rojas, eds. 2002. *El republicanismo en Hispanoamérica: Ensayos de historia intelectual y política*. Mexico City: Fondo de Cultura Económica.

Alda Mejías, Sonia. 2004. "El derecho de elección y de insurrección en Centroamérica: Las revoluciones como medio de garantizar elecciones libres, 1838–1872." In Malamud and Dardé, *Violencia y legitimidad.*

Aljovín de Losada, Cristóbal. 2000. *Caudillos y constituciones: Perú, 1821–1845.* Lima: Pontificia Universidad Católica del Perú/Fondo de Cultura Económica.

Alonso, Paula. 2000. *Between Revolution and the Ballot Box: The Origins of the Argentine Radical Party.* Cambridge: Cambridge University Press.

Annino, Antonio, Luis Castro Leiva, and François-Xavier Guerra, comps. 1994. *De los Imperios a las Naciones.* Zaragoza: Iberoamérica.

Arendt, Hannah. 1990. *On Revolution.* London: Penguin Books.

Aschcraft, Richard. 1987. *Revolutionary Politics and Locke's Two Treatises of Government.* London: Allen and Unwin.

Botana, Natalio, and Ezequiel Gallo. 1997. *De la república posible a la república verdadera (1880–1910).* Buenos Aires: Ariel.

Brading, David. 1991. *The First America: The Spanish Monarchy, Creole Patriots, and the Liberal State, 1492–1867.* Cambridge: Cambridge University Press.

Bragoni, Beatriz. 2010. "Cuyo después de Pavón: Consenso, rebelión y orden político, 1861–1874." In *Un nuevo orden político: Provincias y Estado Nacional, 1852–1880,* edited by Beatriz Bragoni and Eduardo Míguez. Buenos Aires: Biblos.

Buve, Raymond. 1997. "Between Ballots and Bullets: Long-Term Trends in Nineteenth-Century Mexican Political Culture." In *Citizens of the Pyramid: Essays on Mexican Political Culture,* edited by Wil Pansters. Amsterdam: Thela.

Canciani, Leonardo, and Sergio Daghero. 2014. "Dossier: La política y la guerra en perspectiva local; Armas, instituciones y actores sociales en el proceso de construcción del Estado nacional; Argentina (1852–1880)." *Coordenadas: Revista de historia local y regional* 1 (1).

Cañedo Gamboa, Sergio A. 2012. "Ponciano Arriaga and Mariano Ávila's Intellectual Backing of the 14 April 1837 Pronunciamiento of San Luis Potosí." In Fowler, *Malcontents, Rebels, and Pronunciados.*

Carp, E. Wayne. 1987. "The Problem of National Defense in the Early American Republic." In *The American Revolution: Its Character and Limits,* edited by Jack P. Greene. New York: New York University Press.

Centeno, Miguel Ángel. 2002. *Blood and Debt: War and the Nation-State in Latin America.* University Park: Pennsylvania State University Press.

Chambers, Sarah C. 1999. *From Subjects to Citizens: Honor, Gender, and Politics in Arequipa, Peru, 1780–1854.* University Park: Pennsylvania State University Press.

Chiaramonte, José Carlos. 2004. "The Principle of Consent in Latin and Anglo-American Independence." *Journal of Latin American Studies* 36 (3).

———. 2010. *Fundamentos intelectuales y políticos de las independencias: Notas para una nueva historia intelectual de Iberoamérica.* Buenos Aires: Teseo-Colección Instituto Ravignani.

Chust, Manuel. 2005a. "Armed Citizens: The Civic Militia in the Origins of the Mexican National State, 1812–1827." In *The Divine Charter: Constitutionalism and Liberalism in Nineteenth-Century Mexico*, edited by Jaime E. Rodríguez O. Lanham, MD: Rowman and Littlefield.

———. 2005b. "Milicia, milicias y milicianos: Nacionales y cívicos en la formación del Estado-nación mexicano, 1812–1835." In Ortiz Escamilla, *Fuerzas militares en Iberoamérica*.

Chust, Manuel, and Juan Marchena, eds. 2007. *Las armas de la nación: Independencia y ciudadanía en Hispanoamérica (1750–1850)*. Madrid: Iberoamericana.

Chust, Manuel, and José Antonio Serrano Ortega. 2007. "Milicia y revolución liberal en España y en México." In Chust and Marchena, *Las armas de la nación*.

Connaughton, Brian, ed. 2003. *Poder y legitimidad en México en el siglo XIX*. Mexico City: Universidad Autónoma Metropolitana, Unidad Iztapalapa.

Cooper, Jerry. 1997. *The Rise of the National Guard: The Evolution of the American Militia, 1865–1920*. Lincoln: University of Nebraska Press.

Corella Ovares, Esteban. 2012. "El ejército y la guerra en la formación del Estado costarricense." In Garavaglia, Pro Ruiz, and Zimmermann, *Las fuerzas de guerra*.

Cornell, Saul. 2006. *A Well-Regulated Militia: The Founding Fathers and the Origins of Gun Control in America*. New York: Oxford University Press.

Cress, Lawrence Delbert. 1984. "An Armed Community: The Origins and Meaning of the Right to Bear Arms." *Journal of American History* 71 (1).

Cucchi, Laura. 2014. "Entre la 'anarquía' y el 'despotismo': Debates sobre la acción armada y las formas de la contienda política en Córdoba en 1880." *Nuevo Mundo/Mundos Nuevos*, no. 14, École des Hautes Études en Sciences Sociales (EHESS).

Cucchi, Laura, and María José Navajas. 2013. "Garantizar el orden: Debates sobre el derecho de la revolución y el federalismo en el Congreso Nacional durante la intervención a Corrientes en 1878." *PolHis* 11.

Deas, Malcolm. 1993. *Del poder y la gramática, y otros ensayos sobre historia, política y literatura colombianas*. Bogotá: Tercer Mundo Editores.

De la Fuente, Ariel. 2000. *Children of Facundo: Caudillo and Gaucho Insurgency during the Argentine State-Formation Process (La Rioja, 1853–1870)*. Durham, NC: Duke University Press.

De Privitellio, Luciano. 2010. "El ejército entre el cambio de siglo y 1930: Burocratización y nuevos estilos políticos." In AA.VV., *La construcción de la Nación Argentina*.

Deudney, D. H. 1995. "The Philadelphian System: Sovereignty, Arms Control, and Balance of Power in the American States–Union, circa 1787–1861." *International Organization* 49 (2).

Ducey, Michael T. 2004. *A Nation of Villages: Riot and Rebellion in the Mexican Huasteca, 1750–1850*. Tucson: University of Arizona Press.

Earle, Rebecca, ed. 2000. *Rumours of Wars: Civil Conflict in Nineteenth-Century Latin America*. London: Institute of Latin American Studies.

Elias, Norbert. 1994. *The Civilizing Process: Sociogenetic and Psychogenetic Investigations*. Rev. ed. Oxford: Blackwell.

Escalante Gonzalbo, Fernando. 1992. *Ciudadanos imaginarios*. Mexico City: El Colegio de México.

Esquivel Triana, Ricardo. 2008. "La formación militar en Colombia, 1880–1884." In Torres del Río and Rodríguez Hernández, *De milicias reales a militares contrainsurgentes*.

Fernández Abara, Joaquín Rodrigo. 2004. "Los orígenes de la Guardia Nacional y la construcción del ciudadano soldado (Chile, 1823–1833)." *Mapocho* 56.

Flórez Bolívar, Roicer, and Sergio Paolo Solano D. 2011. "Educando al buen ciudadano: Artesanos y Guardias Nacionales en la República de la Nueva Granada (Colombia), 1832–1853." In *Infancia de la Nación: Colombia en el primer siglo de la república*, edited by Sergio Paolo Solano D. and Roicer Flórez Bolívar. Cartagena de Indias: Ediciones Pluma de Mompox.

Forte, Riccardo, and Guillermo Fajardo, eds. 2000. *Consenso y coacción: Estado e instrumentos de control político y social en México y América Latina (siglos xix y XX)*. Mexico City: El Colegio de México/El Colegio Mexiquense.

Fowler, Will. 2009. "El pronunciamiento mexicano del siglo XIX: Hacia una nueva tipología." *Estudios de historia moderna y contemporánea de México* 38 (July–December).

Fowler, Will, ed. 2010. *Forceful Negotiations: The Origins of the Pronunciamiento in Nineteenth-Century Mexico*. Lincoln: University of Nebraska Press.

———. 2012a. *Celebrating Insurrection and Representation of the Nineteenth-Century Mexican Pronunciamiento (The Mexican Experience)*. Lincoln: University of Nebraska Press.

———. 2012b. *Malcontents, Rebels, and Pronunciados: The Politics of Insurrection in Nineteenth-Century Mexico*. Lincoln: University of Nebraska Press.

Fradkin, Raúl. 2006. *La historia de una montonera: Bandolerismo y caudillismo en Buenos Aires, 1826*. Buenos Aires: Siglo XXI.

———. 2012. "Guerra y sociedad en el litoral rioplatense en la primera mitad del siglo XIX." In Garavaglia, Pro Ruiz, and Zimmermann, *Las fuerzas de guerra*.

Frasquet, Ivana. 2007. "El estado armado o la nación en armas: Ejército versus milicia civil en México, 1821–1823." In Chust and Marchena, *Las armas de la nación*.

Gantús, Fausta. 2008. "La inconformidad subversiva: Entre el pronunciamiento y el bandidaje; Un acercamiento a los movimientos rebeldes durante el tuxtepecanismo, 1876–1888." *Estudios de Historia Moderna y Contemporánea de México* 35 (January–June).

Garavaglia, Juan Carlos, Juan Pro Ruiz, and Eduardo Zimmermann, eds. 2012. *Las fuerzas de guerra en la construcción del Estado: América Latina, siglo XIX*. Rosario: Prohistoria ediciones.

Goldman, Noemí, ed. 2008. *Lenguaje y revolución: Conceptos políticos clave en el Río de la Plata, 1780–1850*. Buenos Aires: Prometeo.

González, Fernán E. 2006. "¿Una comunidad política escindida? Guerras civiles y formación del Estado colombiano (1839–1854)." In *Las revoluciones en el mundo atlántico*, edited by María Teresa Calderón and Clément Thibaud. Bogotá: Taurus historia.

Guardino, Peter. 1995. "Barbarism or Republican Law? Guerrero's Peasants and National Politics, 1820–1846." *Hispanic American Historical Review* 75 (2).

———. 2005. *The Time of Liberty: Popular Political Culture in Oaxaca, 1750–1850*. Durham, NC: Duke University Press.

———. 2014. "Gender, Soldiering, and Citizenship in the Mexican-American War of 1846–1848." *American Historical Review* 119 (1).

Guerra, François-Xavier. 1993. "Las metamorfosis de la representación en el siglo xix." In *Democracias posibles: El desafío latinoamericano*, compiled by Georges Couffignal. Buenos Aires: Fondo de Cultura Económica.

———. 2000. "El pronunciamiento en México: Prácticas e imaginarios." *Trace* 37 (June).

Guerrero Domínguez, Ángel Luis. 2007. "*Lex et bellum*: Fuero militar y milicias en el norte del virreinato del Perú a finales del siglo XVIII." In Chust and Marchena, *Las armas de la nación*.

Gutiérrez, Francisco. 1995. *Curso y discurso del movimiento plebeyo, 1849/1854*. Bogotá: El Ancora Editores.

Halperin Donghi, Tulio. 1972. *Revolución y guerra: Formación de una elite dirigente en la Argentina criolla*. Buenos Aires: Siglo XXI.

———. 1975. "Militarización revolucionaria en Buenos Aires, 1806–1815." In *El ocaso del orden colonial en Hispanoamérica*, by Tulio Halperin Donghi. Buenos Aires: Sudamericana.

———. 1980. *Proyecto y construcción de una nación: (Argentina 1846–1880)*. Caracas: Biblioteca de Ayacucho.

———. 1985. *Reforma y disolución de los imperios ibéricos, 1750–1850*. Madrid: Alianza.

Hébrard, Veronique. 2002. "¿Patricio o soldado: Qué 'uniforme' para el ciudadano? El hombre de armas en la construcción de la nación (Venezuela, primera mitad del siglo XIX)." *Revista de Indias* 225.

Hernández Chávez, Alicia. 1989. "Origen y ocaso del ejército porfiriano." *Historia Mexicana* 153 (1).

———. 1993. *La tradición republicana del buen gobierno*. Mexico City: Fideicomiso de Historia de las Américas de El Colegio de México/Fondo de Cultura Económica.

———. 2007. "La Guardia Nacional en la construcción del orden republicano." In Chust and Marchena, *Las armas de la nación*.

Hernández López, Conrado. 2006. "'Espíritu de cuerpo' y el papel del ejército permanente en el surgimiento del estado-nación, 1821–1860." *Ulúa: Revista de historia, sociedad y cultura* 8 (July–December).

———. 2007. "Juárez y los militares (1855–1867)." In *Las rupturas de Juárez*, by Conrado Hernández López and Israel Arroyo. Oaxaca: Universidad Autónoma Benito Juárez/Universidad Autónoma Metropolitana.

———. 2008. "Las fuerzas armadas durante la Guerra de Reforma (1856–1867)." *Signos históricos* 19 (January–June).

Hernández Ponce, Roberto. 1984. "La Guardia Nacional de Chile: Apuntes sobre su origen y organización, 1808–1848." *Historia* 19.

Herrera, Ricardo. 2015. *For Liberty and the Republic: The American Citizen as Soldier, 1775–1861*. New York: New York University Press.

Hirsch, Leonardo. 2012. "Entre la 'revolución' y la 'evolución': Las movilizaciones del Noventa." *PolHis* 9.

Irurozqui, Marta. 2000. *"A bala, piedra y palo": La construcción de la ciudadanía política en Bolivia, 1826–1952*. Sevilla: Diputación de Sevilla.

———. 2003. "El bautismo de la violencia: Indígenas patriotas en la revolución de 1870 en Bolivia." In *Identidad, ciudadanía y participación popular desde la colonia al siglo XX*, edited by Josefa Salmón and Guillermo Delgado. La Paz: Editores Plural.

———. 2004. *La ciudadanía en debate en América Latina: Discusiones historiográficas y una propuesta teórica sobre el valor público de la infracción electoral*. Lima: Instituto de Estudios Peruanos (Documento de Trabajo no. 139).

———. 2009. "Muerte en El Loreto: Ciudadanía armada y violencia política en Bolivia (1861–1862)." *Revista de Indias* 246 (May–August).

Irwin, Domingo, and Ingrid Micett. 2008. *Caudillos, militares y poder: Una historia del pretorianismo en Venezuela*. Caracas: Universidad Católica Andrés Bello.

Jacobsen, Nils, and Cristóbal Aljovín, eds. 2005. *Political Culture in the Andes, 1750s–1950s*. Durham, NC: Duke University Press.

Keane, John. 1996. *Reflections on Violence*. London: Verso.

Macías, Flavia. 2003. "Ciudadanía armada, identidad nacional y estado provincial: Tucumán, 1854–1870." In *La vida política en la Argentina del siglo XIX: Armas, votos y voces*, edited by Hilda Sabato and Alberto Lettieri. Buenos Aires: Fondo de Cultura Económica.

———. 2007a. "De 'cívicos' a 'guardias nacionales': Un análisis del componente militar en el proceso de construcción de la ciudadanía; Tucumán, 1840–1860." In Chust and Marchena, *Las armas de la nación*.

———. 2007b. "Violencia y política facciosa en el norte argentino: Tucumán en la década de 1860." *Boletín Americanista* 57.

———. 2014. *Armas y política en la Argentina: Tucumán, siglo XIX*. Madrid: Consejo Superior de Investigaciones Científicas.

Macías, Flavia, and Hilda Sabato. 2013. "La Guardia Nacional: Estado, política y uso de la fuerza en la Argentina de la segunda mitad del siglo XIX." *PolHis* 11 (September).

Malamud, Carlos. 1998. "La restauración del orden: Represión y amnistía en las revoluciones argentinas de 1890 y 1893." In Posada Carbó, *In Search of a New Order*.

Malamud, Carlos, ed. 2000. *Legitimidad, representación y alternancia en España y América Latina: Las reformas electorales, 1880–1930*. Mexico City: Fideicomiso Historia de las Américas de El Colegio de México/Fondo de Cultura Económica.

Malamud, Carlos, and Carlos Dardé, eds. 2004. *Violencia y legitimidad: Política y revoluciones en España y América Latina, 1840–1910*. Santander: Universidad de Cantabria.

Mallon, Florencia. 1995. *Peasant and Nation: The Making of Postcolonial Mexico and Peru*. Berkeley: University of California Press.

Marchena, Juan, and Manuel Chust, eds. 2008. *Por la fuerza de las armas: Ejército e independencias en Iberoamérica*. Castellón de la Plana: Universitat Jaume I.

Mayer, Arno. 2000. *The Furies: Violence and Terror in the French and Russian Revolutions*. Princeton, NJ: Princeton University Press.

McEvoy, Carmen. 1997. *La utopía republicana: Ideales y realidades en la formación de la cultura política peruana (1871–1919)*. Lima: Pontificia Universidad Católica del Perú.

McEvoy, Carmen, and Ana María Stuven, eds. 2007. *La república peregrina: Hombres de armas y letras en América del Sur, 1800–1884*. Lima: Instituto de Estudios Peruanos/Instituto Francés de Estudios Andinos.

Méndez, Cecilia. 2005. *The Plebeian Republic: The Huanta Rebellion and the Making of the Peruvian State, 1820–1850*. Durham, NC: Duke University Press.

———. 2006. "Las paradojas del autoritarismo: Ejército, campesinado y etnicidad en el Perú; Siglos XIX al XXI." *Íconos: Revista de Ciencias Sociales*, no. 26 (Quito).

Metzger, Jan. 1999. *Die Milizarmee in klassischen Republikanismus: Die Odyssee eines militärpolitischen Konzeptes von Florenz über England und Schottland nach Nordamerika (15.–18. Jahrhundert)*. Bern: P. Haupt.

Míguez, Eduardo. 2011. *Mitre montonero: La Revolución de 1874 y las formas de la política en la organización nacional*. Buenos Aires: Sudamericana.

Morgan, Edmund. 1988. *Inventing the People: The Rise of Popular Sovereignty in England and America*. New York: W. W. Norton.

Mücke, Ulrich. 2004. *Political Culture in Nineteenth-Century Peru: The Rise of the Partido Civil*. Pittsburgh: University of Pittsburgh Press.

Muehlbauer, Matthew S., and David J. Ulbrich. 2014. *Ways of War: American Military History from the Colonial Era to the Twenty-First Century*. New York: Routledge.

Negretto, Gabriel, and José Antonio Aguilar Rivera. 2000. "Rethinking the Legacy of the Liberal State in Latin America: The Cases of Argentina (1853–1916) and Mexico (1857–1910)." *Journal of Latin American Studies* 32 (2).

Ortiz Escamilla, Juan, ed. 2005. *Fuerzas militares en Iberoamérica, siglos XVIII y XIX*. Mexico City: El Colegio de México; Zamora, Michoacán: El Colegio de Michoacán; Jalapa, Veracruz: Universidad Veracruzana.

Palti, Elías. 2007. *El tiempo de la política: El siglo XIX reconsiderado*. Buenos Aires: Siglo XXI.

Patiño Villa, Carlos Alberto. 2010. *Guerra y construcción del Estado en Colombia, 1810–2010*. Bogotá: Universidad Militar Nueva Granada.

Peralta Ruiz, Víctor. 1999. "El mito del ciudadano armado: La 'Semana Magna'? y las elecciones de 1844 en Lima." In Sabato, *Ciudadanía política y formación de las naciones*.

Pinto Vallejos, Julio, and Verónica Valdivia Ortiz de Zárate. 2009. *¿Chilenos todos? La construcción social de la nación (1810–1840)*. Santiago: LOM ediciones.

Pinzón de Lewin, Patricia. 1994. *El ejército y las elecciones: Ensayo histórico*. Bogotá: CEREC.

Poole, Deborah, ed. 1994. *Unruly Order: Violence, Power, and Cultural Identity in the High Provinces of Southern Peru*. Boulder, CO: Westview Press.

Posada Carbó, Eduardo, ed. 1996. *Elections before Democracy: The History of Elections in Europe and Latin America*. London: Macmillan.

———. 1998. *In Search of a New Order: Essays on the Politics and Society of Nineteenth-Century Latin America*. London: Institute of Latin American Studies.

Prado Arellano, Luis Ervin. 2008. "Ejército republicano y control social en las provincias del Cauca, 1830–1850." In Torres del Río and Rodríguez Hernández, *De milicias reales a militares contrainsurgentes*.

Rabinovich, Alejandro. 2013a. "Milicias, ejércitos y guerras." In *Historia de la Provincia de Buenos Aires: De la organización provincial a la federalización de Buenos Aires (1821–1880)*, edited by Marcela Ternavasio. Buenos Aires: Universidad Pedagógica/Editorial Edhasa.

———. 2013b. *La société guerrière: Pratiques, discours et valeurs militaires dans le Rio de la Plata, 1806–1852*. Rennes: Presses Universitaires de Rennes.

Rangel Silva, José Alfredo. 2007. "Milicias en el oriente de San Luis Potosí, 1793–1823." In Chust and Marchena, *Las armas de la nación*.

Rosanvallon, Pierre. 1992. *Le sacré du citoyen: Histoire du suffrage universel en France*. Paris: Gallimard.

———. 1998. *Le peuple introuvable: Histoire de la représentation démocratique en France*. Paris: Gallimard.

Sabato, Hilda. 2001a. "El ciudadano en armas: Violencia política en Buenos Aires, 1852–1890." In *Kultur-Diskurs: Kontinuität und Wandel der Diskussion um Indentitäten in Lateinamerika im 19. und 20. Jahrhundert*, edited by Michael Riekenberg, Stefan Rinke, and Peer Schmidt. Stuttgart: Heinz.

———. 2001b. "On Political Citizenship in Nineteenth-Century Latin America." *American Historical Review* 106 (4).

———. 2008a. *Buenos Aires en armas: La revolución de 1880*. Buenos Aires: Siglo XXI.

———. 2008b. "Milicias, ciudadanía y revolución: El ocaso de una tradición política. Argentina, 1880." *Ayer: Revista de Historia Contemporánea* 70 (Madrid).

———. 2009. "'Resistir la imposición': Revolución, ciudadanía y república en la Argentina de 1880." *Revista de Indias* 246 (May–August).

———. 2016. "Milicias en Hispanoamérica: Apuntes para una historia." In *América Latina: De la independencia a la crisis del liberalismo, 1810–1930,* edited by Nuria Tabanera and Marta Bonaudo. Madrid: Marcial Pons; Zaragoza: Prensas de la Universidad de Zaragoza.

Sabato, Hilda, ed. 1999. *Ciudadanía política y formación de las naciones: Perspectivas históricas de América Latina.* Mexico City: Fideicomiso de Historia de las Américas de El Colegio de México/Fondo de Cultura Económica.

Salvatore, Ricardo. 2003. *Wandering Paysanos: State Order and Subaltern Experience in Buenos Aires during the Rosas Era.* Durham, NC: Duke University Press.

Sanders, James E. 2004. *Contentious Republicans: Popular Politics, Race, and Class in Nineteenth-Century Colombia.* Durham, NC: Duke University Press.

———. 2010. "Subaltern Strategies of Citizenship and Soldiering in Colombia's Civil Wars: Afro- and Indigenous Colombians' Experiences in the Cauca, 1851–1877." In *Military Struggle and Identity Formation in Latin America: Race, Nation, and Community during the Liberal Period,* edited by Nicola Foote and René Harder Horst. Gainesville: University Press of Florida.

Santoni, Pedro. 1988. "A Fear of the People: The Civic Militia of Mexico in 1845." *Hispanic American Historical Review* 68 (2).

———. 1996. "The Failure of Mobilization: The Civic Militia of Mexico in 1846." *Mexican Studies/Estudios Mexicanos,* 12, 2.

———. 2002. "'Where Did the Other Heroes Go?' Exalting the *Polko* National Guard Battalions in Nineteenth-Century Mexico." *Journal of Latin American Studies* 34.

Serrano Ortega, José Antonio. 1999. "Liberalismo gaditano y milicias cívicas en Guanajuato, 1820–1836." In *La construcción de la legitimidad política en México,* edited by Brian Connaughton, Carlos Illades, and Sonia Pérez Toledo. Zamora, Michoacán: El Colegio de Michoacán; Mexico City: Universidad Autónoma Metropolitana/Universidad Nacional Autónoma de México/El Colegio de México.

Sobrevilla Perea, Natalia. 2007. "'Ciudadanos armados': Las Guardias Nacionales en la construcción de la nación en el Perú de mediados del siglo XIX." In Chust and Marchena, *Las armas de la nación.*

———. 2009. "Batallas por la legitimidad: Constitucionalismo y conflicto político en el Perú del siglo (1812–1860)." *Revista de Indias* 246 (May–August).

———. 2010. "Colored by the Past: The Birth of the Armed Forces in Republican Peru." *Estudios Interdisciplinarios de América Latina y el Caribe* 22 (1).

Straka, Tomás. 2009. "La república revolucionaria: La idea de revolución en el pensamiento político venezolano del siglo XIX." *Revista Politeia* 32 (43).

Thibaud, Clément. 2006. *Républiques en armes: Les armées de Bolívar dans les guerres d'indépendence du Venezuela et de la Colombie*. Rennes: Presses Universitaires de Rennes.

———. 2007. "Des républiques en armes à la république armée: Guerre révolutionaire, fédéralisme et centralisme au Venezuela et en Nouvelle-Grenade, 1808–1830." *Annales Historiques de la Révolution Française* 2.

Thomson, Guy. 1990. "Bulwarks of Patriotic Liberalism: The National Guard, Philharmonic Corps, and Patriotic Juntas in Mexico, 1847–88." *Journal of Latin American Studies* 22 (1).

———. 1998. "Order through Insurrection: The Rise of the District of Tetela during Mexico's Liberal Revolution, 1854–1876." In Posada Carbó, *In Search of a New Order*.

———. 2007. "Citizens in Search of a State: Popular Embodiments of Military Institutions in the Nineteenth-Century Hispanic World." Paper presented at the Conference on "Citizenship, Revolutions, and Political Violence in the Formation of the Latin American Republics," Center of Latin American Studies, Stanford University, Stanford, California, April.

———. 2010. "¿Convivencia o conflicto? Guerra, etnia y nación en el México del siglo XIX." In *Nación, Constitución y Reforma, 1821–1908*, edited by Erika Pani. Mexico City: CIDE/Fondo de Cultura Económica.

———. 2012. "The End of the 'Catholic Nation': Reform and Reaction in Puebla, 1854–1856." In Fowler, *Malcontents, Rebels, and Pronunciados*.

Thomson, Guy, with David LaFrance. 1999. *Patriotism, Politics, and Popular Liberalism in Nineteenth-Century Mexico: Juan Francisco Lucas and the Puebla Sierra*. Wilmington, DE: Scholarly Resources.

Titto, Ricardo de, ed. 2009. *El pensamiento de Bartolomé Mitre y los liberales*. Buenos Aires: Editorial El Ateneo.

Torres del Río, César, and Saúl Rodríguez Hernández, eds. 2008. *De milicias reales a militares contrainsurgentes: La institución militar en Colombia del siglo XVIII al XXI*. Bogotá: Pontificia Universidad Javeriana.

Valenzuela, J. Samuel. 1985. *Democratización vía reforma: La expansión del sufragio en Chile*. Buenos Aires: Ediciones del Instituto de Desarrollo Económico y Social (IDES).

Vázquez, Josefina Z. 1998. "Milicia y ejército: Punto de fricción entre el poder local y el poder nacional." In *Nation Building in Nineteenth-Century Latin America*, edited by Hans-Joachim König and Marianne Wiesebron. Leiden: Leiden University.

Velasco Herrera, Viviana. 2012. "Ejército y milicias del Estado ecuatoriano, 1830–1861." In Garavaglia, Pro Ruiz, and Zimmermann, *Las fuerzas de guerra*.

Walker, Charles F. 1989. "Montoneros, bandoleros, malhechores: Criminalidad y política en las primeras décadas republicanas." *Pasado y Presente* 2.

———. 1999. *Smoldering Ashes: Cuzco and the Creation of Republican Peru, 1780–1840*. Durham, NC: Duke University Press.

Whisker, James B. 1992. *The Militia*. Lewiston, NY: Edwin Mellen Press.

Williams, Raymond. 1983. *Keywords*. New York: Oxford University Press.

Wood, James. 2002. "The Burden of Citizenship: Artisans, Elections, and the Fuero Militar in Santiago de Chile, 1822–1851." *The Americas* 58 (3).

———. 2011. *The Society of Equality: Popular Republicanism and Democracy in Santiago de Chile, 1818–1851*. Albuquerque: University of New Mexico Press.

Wolf, Justin. 2010. "Soldiers and Statesmen: Race, Liberalism, and the Paradoxes of Afro-Nicaraguan Military Service, 1844–1863." In *Military Struggle and Identity Formation in Latin America: Race, Nation, and Community during the Liberal Period*, edited by Nicola Foote and René Harder Horst. Gainesville: University Press of Florida.

Zermeño Padilla, Guillermo. 2014. *Revolución*, vol. 9 of the *Diccionario político y social del mundo iberomericano*. Madrid: Universidad del País Vasco/Iberconceptos/Centro de Estudios Políticos y Constitucionales.

Zimmermann, Eduardo. 2010. "La justicia federal frente a los levantamientos provinciales, 1860–1880." In *Un nuevo orden político: Provincias y Estado Nacional, 1852–1880*, edited by Beatriz Bragoni and Eduardo Míguez. Buenos Aires: Biblos.

———. 2012. "Guerra, fuerzas militares y construcción estatal en el Río de la Plata, siglo XIX." In Garavaglia, Pro Ruiz, and Zimmermann, *Las fuerzas de guerra*.

CHAPTER FOUR

Public Opinion

FROM THE VERY dawn of the revolutionary movements, *public opinion* became a crucial concept in the political life of Spanish America. Widely used in eighteenth-century Europe to discuss the foundation of authority, it soon migrated to America where it also "came to function as . . . the abstract source of legitimacy in a transformed political culture."[1] Central to the republican rhetoric and practices of the nineteenth century, that key "political invention" acquired changing meanings, all of which ultimately referred to the exercise of popular control over government.[2] In the context of the replacement of the divine right of kings for popular sovereignty, the early revolutionary elites of Spanish America considered the voice of the people embodied in *public opinion*—as well as in the suffrage—as a basic pillar of political legitimacy. From then on, and regardless of the different definitions proposed since the term first emerged in political language, it was an unavoidable reference in the construction and contestation of power. And it opened the way to debates over its nature, as well as to claims regarding who—which persons, groups, or institutions—best represented or expressed it. Rather than exploring what were the meanings attributed to public opinion, this chapter will look at how this political invention opened the way to the development and articulation of a series of institutions and practices that played an important part in the nineteenth-century republics, not least as a space of participation for different sectors of the population in the political life of the period.

The Voice of the People

In the decades that followed the revolutions of independence, the emerging political leaderships considered *public opinion* to be the rational expression of the will of the citizens, whose existence was tied to the coming to being of the modern individual, free from traditional and corporate bonds. It was also related to the creation of new forms of sociability, to the spread of associations and of a periodical press, which presumably represented public opinion. In view of promoting their development—in a world that until then had seen very little of that—freedom of the press and of association were on the agenda of most of the first republican administrations. They also actively participated in the creation of an official and quasi-official press, and of associations that mainly targeted the educated few. While the public cherished by the enlightened elites was an abstract public, of rational and modern individuals, the turbulent postrevolutionary years witnessed the emergence of different groups and sectors that voiced their own claims in the name of very concrete publics, often quite different from the blueprint proposed from above. Also, previous forms of sociability, like the artisan guilds (*gremios*) and the religious confraternities (*cofradías*) continued to play a part in representing and voicing collective concerns. The use of public spaces was, perhaps, where old and new forms merged more easily, as the colorful street celebrations of patriotic events staged by the new authorities had much in common with the former tradition of popular feasts and religious pageants. Also, these were sites for the display of protest and unrest.

The driving forces for the expansion of public means of expression and action resulted from a combination of government and elite initiatives ("from above") and those originating in the social realm ("from below"). The upsurge of a relatively autonomous public is usually considered to be both cause and effect of the consolidation of a civil society and of a public sphere.[3] In fact, during the second half of the century, the network of civic institutions grew and diversified in Spanish America, particularly in those cities where the social fabric was becoming increasingly complex—from Buenos Aires to Mexico, Arequipa, and Santiago de Chile. There was a remarkable multiplication of associations of all sorts—mutual aid societies, social clubs, Masonic lodges, learned societies, and so on—while a vigorous and increasingly independent press developed and found a relatively enlarged readership. All of these did not only represent, protect, and look after the interests and opinions of their originating constituencies, they actually helped to shape their respective publics. At the same time, they created a thick web of relations and interactions among the different groups and sectors of society and engaged in exchanges and disputes with one another and with the state and government institutions. These developments did not preclude the expansion of other, more informal, mechanisms of sociability, both old and new, and the subsistence of more traditional institutions and practices. In these ways, different groups and sectors of the population defined their interests, voiced their opinions, and represented their claims through their organizations and newspapers, and also more directly, by displaying a physical presence in the civic spaces of the cities and mobilizing in large numbers.

The abstract notion of *public opinion* and the concrete formation and display of heterogeneous, and oftentimes conflicting voices and actions that claimed to represent the will of "the people" in general or of specific publics in particular, are two distinct although tightly related aspects of the politics of the age of revolution and beyond. The first one refers to the new foundations of authority in regimes increasingly based upon the principle of popular sovereignty. The second, in turn, has to do with the social transformations that were taking place in the same polities as well as with the institutional changes put forward by the political leadership in order to give shape to a concrete public opinion needed for the legitimation of power. Scholars have offered different hypotheses as to which came first and what were the final causes of each (or both) of these developments. Far from attempting to advance in any one of these directions, the following pages will focus on the examination of the actual mechanisms of people's involvement and participation in the polity related to the broad field of *public opinion*. These varied greatly according to time and place, but they were always a key component in the political life of the new republics.

Forms of Sociability Old and New

In late colonial Spanish America, the ancien régime landscape experienced social and cultural transformations that were not out of tune with similar events in the metropolis and the neighboring France and England. In a more reduced scale than in France and England, during the eighteenth century, the ideas and proposals of the Enlightenment circulated throughout the Spanish empire and inspired the introduction of new political notions, such as public opinion, and the creation of new forms of sociability that challenged the traditional ways of association and collective action. While these were based on ascription and custom, and functioned according to strongly hierarchic established conventions, the novel ones were presumably set up on a voluntary basis by free and equal individuals brought together by a common purpose and the will to deliberate and dialogue among equals in an atmosphere only governed by the laws of reason. Scholars discuss the extent, pace, and consequences of these changes in metropolitan Spain and compare them with experiences in other countries, and they differ on whether or not similar developments took place at the same time in the colonies. Among them, François-Xavier Guerra was probably the first one to propose a wide-ranging interpretation of these innovations both sides of the Spanish Atlantic. In line with the views that Augustin Cochin and François Furet had put forward for France, Guerra found in the expansion of modern forms of sociability the key to the cultural change that was at the heart of the transition to political modernity. This process came earlier in the metropolis than in the colonies, he argues, where it gained speed only around the imperial crisis of the first decade of the nineteenth century.[4]

In any case, and regardless of how widespread the new practices were in different places of Spanish America during the eighteenth century, they certainly expanded on the eve of independence, when all the main cities witnessed the creation of forms of modern sociability and a periodical press, led mainly by members of the lettered classes. The notion of public opinion gained weight during the years of the revolutions, and different social and political actors resorted to various means, both old and new, to raise their voice and claim their share in the debates and decisions regarding the current political crisis. What followed after these convulsionary years was not a smooth or straightforward path to the consolidation of those novel institutions and practices, but rather a multifaceted process of definition, creation, contestation, and overlapping of different forms of public expression and action. After the demise of colonial rule, and in the context of the formation of the new polities, public opinion secured its place in the political rhetoric of the incoming regimes. But within this framework, the actual patterns of engagement in collective practices with public resonance are better portrayed through the metaphor recently proposed by Nils Jacobsen of "a multicolored web in a tattered cloth" than by any classification of them in terms of their "traditional" or "modern" traits.[5] This was also a rapidly changing web with no clear-cut tendency toward systematic expansion or contraction.

THE ASSOCIATIVE CREED

The novel associative creed that had timidly found some adepts in the late colonial era, in a context of clear predominance of more traditional forms of sociability, experienced a sudden boost during the first two decades of the nineteenth century, particularly in the main urban focuses of the revolutions. *Tertulias* (a local version of the salons), patriotic societies, secret lodges, and other more informal groupings sprung up in various places and served as a breeding ground for enlightened values, revolutionary ideas, and political initiatives.

After independence, the previous impetus seemed to wane, although the attraction for modern forms of sociability on the part of the enlightened circles was there to stay. For them, the new associations were vital for the advancement of civility and civic life, in short, for contributing to "civilization." They therefore played an active role in promoting that type of social and cultural endeavors with uneven results in terms of numbers, duration, and membership. The rather informal *tertulias* and *salones* survived as sites for conversation, entertainment, dancing, and cultural exchanges. Mostly held in the homes of distinguished families in the larger cities, and often hosted by the lady of the house, these regular gatherings were apparently less demanding in terms of etiquette and intellectual tournaments than their French relative, the *salon*, but they always required the display of civil manners, disposition for informed dialogue, and evidence of good taste. Coffeehouses, in turn, expanded as a space of male sociability that often served as a meeting place for reading and debating public affairs. At the same time, more formal instances of sociability such as literary and learned societies, educational groups, and professional circles found only limited expansion during these decades. Every important city, from Buenos Aires to Mexico, witnessed the creation of some such institutions, considered by their promoters to be a school of civility and a beacon of modernity in a predominantly traditional milieu. Typically, they were established following the up-to-date codes of equality among members, freedom of speech and exchanges, and self-rule. Patriotic societies and philanthropic associations had a similar development, but in this case oftentimes the initiative came directly "from above," from the local or national governments that pushed forward this type of organization.

In fact, during the first half of the century the vitality of associations in general owed much to the efforts and active involvement of reformist governments. Thus, for example, in the 1820s and early 1830s in Buenos Aires and Mexico, there was an official impulse to expand civil liberties as well as to encourage or directly organize associations. Administrations that, on the contrary, mistrusted the novelties of the age, valued a unitary view of public opinion, or felt threatened by other forces, tended to curtail these activities. To go back to Buenos Aires:

in the 1830s, with the ascent to power of opposition leader Juan Manuel de Rosas, continuity on these matters marked the succession of Bernardino Rivadavia's period of liberal reforms, but ten years later the same regime tightened its grip in order to dismantle most of the elite associative practices, exert control over all forms of sociability, and restrain public expressions of dissent. The 1840s marked also a low point for Mexico, but in this case mainly due to the problems brought about by the war with the United States. In both cases, the tendency reversed in the following years, with a rapid and widespread increase in public life.

Associations' public engagement turned them into actors of the political realm. Yet contemporaries did not approve of the organization of specifically political forms of sociability in view of competing for power (see chapter 2). Activity in this regard took place mainly through informal networks and was connected to partisan initiative and action. A paradoxical result of such mistrust for divisive politics was that, in the absence of specific mechanisms to channel it, partisan rivalries came to permeate the associative world at large, which oftentimes mirrored, nurtured, and reproduced the cleavages and frictions of the political realm. In the first decades after independence, the creation of secret societies—sometimes Masonic lodges—to operate in that realm offers an example of the overlapping of the civic and the political associative practices. The Mexican electoral confrontations of the 1820s offer the best-known example (but not the only one) of this intersection; two large Masonic groups engaged in partisan competition and led the disputes for power by actively participating in public debate, recruiting followers, and mobilizing voters for their respective factions.

Up to the 1840s, the associative drive was basically limited to the modernizing sectors of the privileged classes mainly lo-

cated in the larger cities. In some cases, however, these organizations extended their appeal to broader groups of the urban
population, and thus expanded the reach of the new creed.
Their influence was weaker among the lower classes as well as
in the rural areas, where other forms of sociability prevailed.
The Catholic Church exerted a decisive role in this regard, and
religious brotherhoods and confraternities attracted men and
women from very different social sectors, ethnic backgrounds,
and places of residence. Artisan guilds of colonial origin, as
well as communal institutions, remained a familiar feature in
the Spanish American landscape, together with more informal
sites of popular exchanges, like taverns (*pulperías*, *pulquerías*,
chicherías, and such), country fairs, and markets.

In practice, old and new forms often coexisted, overlapped,
or combined in different ways. At the same time, republican
rhetoric insisted upon the distinction between the traditional
and the modern, while the impact of the associative doctrine
went well beyond those directly involved in the novel associations. It was their public visibility, their activism, and their role
in the realm of "public opinion" that turned them into noticeable
actors of the political scene. This presence did not result, however, in any systematic expansion; rather, in most of the known
cases, periods of growth in the number of associations and their
membership alternated with periods of contraction, depending
mostly on the political situation and the government attitude
toward such forms of social and cultural organization.

ASSOCIATIVE FERVOR

Around midcentury, this picture began to change in the context of important social, economic, and political transformations experienced by most of the Spanish American republics.
Starting in the late 1840s, there was a remarkable expansion of

voluntary associations of all sorts that continued throughout the rest of the century. This tendency no longer depended mainly upon government initiatives and the will of the enlightened few, and although official policies and elite support continued to play a part in the development of the novel forms of sociability, the main driving force came from an increasingly autonomous civil society. More and more, associations were established and run by men (and, to a much lesser extent, women) from different social and cultural backgrounds who understood them as effective means of self-organization for different purposes.

In the 1850s, the political success of the so-called liberals in several Spanish American republics brought about, among other important measures, a renewed commitment to civil liberties. Freedom of the press and of association became widely acclaimed, and most administrations passed regulations to establish their scope and limitations. This normative swing together with the increasing appeal of certain strands of liberalism that emphasized political equality and citizens' participation in public life created a favorable context for the renewed enthusiasm in voluntary associations. "The association is the idea that marches at the avant-garde of universal civilization"— those words, pronounced by the president of the Argentine Sociedad Tipográfica Bonaerense in 1862, express a conviction that was widely held at the time. Leaders of the republican movements and the 1848 revolutions in Europe proclaimed fraternity as a key value of social organization, a doctrine that found adepts and original representatives in Latin America. For them, voluntary associations were the ideal sites for the construction of a free, fraternal, and republican society. Thus, these were not just a school for civilized manners, as their enlightened predecessors had claimed, but also a space for the breeding and practice of republican virtues.

Despite criticism of this ideology from different quarters, it was at the heart of much of the associative fervor post-1850s. Hundreds of initiatives sprung up and developed in towns and cities all over Spanish America, as well as, if to a lesser extent, in rural villages. The region witnessed the establishment of mutual aid societies; immigrants' associations; literary circles; scientific and learned societies; Masonic lodges; professional groups; philharmonic bodies; social, cultural, and sports clubs; philanthropic organizations; merchants' and business associations; festive groups; and more ephemeral committees for the pursue of specific, short-term, objectives.

According to Carlos Forment's overall figures for Mexico, around 1,400 "civic associations" were founded between 1857 and 1881, half of which sprung up in the last decade of that period. In Peru, numbers are lower, and Forment finds 350 between 1856 and 1885, although they meant a significant increase from the very few (a couple of dozen at the most) in the first half of the century.[6] No equivalent published data are available for Argentina, but after the declining activity of the 1840s, contemporary observers talk about an "explosion" of associations in the 1850s, which did not decline in the following decades. By the 1880s, two hundred mutual aid societies existed in Buenos Aires alone, a city where voluntary associations of all sorts found fertile ground for expansion. The rest of the country also witnessed a systematic increase of associative life. Colombia and Chile, in turn, register a burgeoning movement in the same direction, and while we have few specific studies of this topic for other areas, there are some indications that the trend reached most countries of the region.

Associations came to operate as a wide net of connections whereby different groups of people could meet specific needs; build personal links of belonging and solidarity; define, redefine, and represent collective and individual interests; perform cultural, festive, and recreational activities; and display their presence, opinions, and claims in the public sphere. At the same time, these organizations usually transcended their specific aims and became part of the larger, "progressive" and "civilizing" associative movement. Within this context, although diversity was the rule, it is possible to point to certain shared features and trends.

In most of Spanish America, people from very different sectors of the population joined the associative movement. Within this diversity, however, participation was highest among men from the urban areas, large cities in the first place but also lesser towns. Women were often formally excluded or relegated to the margins, although in some organizations—such as philanthropic societies—they occupied leading roles. Membership followed different social patterns, but these were seldom defined strictly in terms of class, as most associations included men and women belonging to different levels of the social spectrum. Workers' mutual aid societies—of great importance during this period—are an interesting case in point. Scholars have seen them as the direct antecedent of labor-movement organizations of the late nineteenth century, and although there are some grounds to back up this argument, their prevailing ideological frameworks, their institutional structure, and the place they occupied in public life were quite different from those of later labor associations. Most mutual aid societies defined their objectives and functions in terms of the protection and defense of work and of workers—of all levels, from masters to apprentices—of a particular trade, craft, or profession. They projected a highly positive image of labor as the engine of a productive social life, and of formal workers as the embodiment of republican virtues. In contrast, those who did not fit into this image were cast as parasites, a label that not only applied to those members of the upper echelons of society who did not need to work for a living, but also to those who belonged to its lowest levels and did not qualify to join the ranks of the formal workers. In accordance with this general view, mutual aid societies enlisted all members of the corresponding trade or profession, considered as "workers" who performed productive tasks, regardless of their position in the social hierarchy. Thus, for example, the *sociedades tipográficas* (typographical societies), which were always among the first and more active societies in the period, included all those in printing jobs and positions, from the directors and editors of newspapers to the lowest rank of laborers involved in the press. And analogous coverage prevailed in other trades.

A similar type of socially ample recruitment was observed by mutual aid societies organized by immigrants, which mostly sought to attract members from various echelons of their respective national groups. In this case, the selection was made on cultural and ethnic grounds, in ways that were themselves subject to controversy. Thus, for example, in the case of the Argentine numerous associations created by immigrants, the first and largest mutual aid societies defined their target constituencies in very broad terms to include all members of a particular nation, that is, Spain, France, Italy. In the case of the pioneer "Italian" societies in Buenos Aires, they came into being well before the unification of Italy, so that their definition was, in itself, a political program: they strove for a united nation and promoted that identity among immigrants who actually came from regions formally dependent upon other European states. The men who led these associations sought to recruit members from different parts of the peninsula to give shape to a unified "Italian" community in Argentina. The Spanish mutual aid movement, in turn, also privileged the broad national definition, although later in the century the regional and local approach gained increasing favor among immigrants and their leadership, and resulted in a competition between the Spanish affiliation and more restricted regional identities. In all of these cases, however, membership was socially diverse.

Other institutions, like Masonic lodges, patriotic societies, philharmonic groups, sport clubs, literary circles, and even some of the professional circles, also showed diversity in their composition. This was a relatively inclusive pattern, but far from universal; in each case, membership cut across parts of the social spectrum, but there were always limitations and exclusions. And in some cases, such as social clubs and business organizations, among others, these amounted to highly selective restrictions.

Associations of very different kinds shared a common trust in organization, and most of them adhered to a presumably democratic set of functioning rules. Equality of rights among members, free periodical elections to choose the authorities, and founding statutes that regulated all institutional operations were the basic pillars of associative practices. The egalitarian principle did not preclude, however, the forging and solidification of internal hierarchies, which generated and reproduced unequal relations within most institutions. Case studies of associations in different countries also show that leadership was frequently concentrated, and that although ascent to the top positions was often related to the possession of social and cultural capital, it was basically dependent on the capacity to operate politically both inside the institution and outward, in the public realm.

In fact, associations played a key role in public life. Most of them went well beyond their specific purposes to participate in larger public debates and actions. These institutions and their leaderships defined shared fields of dialogue, circulation, exchange, and competition and gave shape to an associative movement that spoke in the name of the public as a whole and interacted with other institutions and actors of the public realm. Despite this overall involvement, associations usually prided themselves on being "apolitical" and banned partisan involvement from their premises. The contrast between the virtues of civil society and the corruption of political life was a recurrent topic in the language of the times. Thus, in the name of their civic aspiration to pursue the common good, associations shared the widespread distrust in current politics and the partisan world. This declared partisan abstention, however, was repeatedly overlooked in practice, and although the apolitical rhetoric was strongly upheld in statutes and declarations, actual political connections, involvement, and disputes were a recurring feature of these institutions.

These associative practices gained momentum as the century advanced and continued to coexist, overlap, and sometimes even merge, with other, more traditional ways of sociability and collective action. The older forms did not, however, remain unchanged, or isolated in their own social or cultural niches. Communal organizations in rural areas—indigenous and others—Catholic *hermandades* and *cofradías*, and other such organizations, as well as more informal means of sociability (market, fairs, pubs) were part of the larger picture of institutions whose voices and actions had public resonances. And although not all of them weighed the same in a public realm where power was unevenly distributed, they did belong to the shared, albeit heterogeneous, "multicolored web" so perceptively portrayed by Nils Jacobsen for Peru.

The Press

THE BIRTH OF A PRINT CULTURE

Print culture and newspapers were pivotal in the political transformations that took place on both sides of the Atlantic during the revolutionary era and beyond. From then on, the periodical press had a decisive role in all polities governed by the principle of popular sovereignty. Not least in Spanish America. It featured as the main actor in most histories of the imperial crisis and the movements toward independence and remained an important player in the accounts of the republican era. More so than associations, the press owed its prestige to its role in the embodiment of public opinion, that key dimension of modern politics. And throughout the nineteenth century, it became a vital piece in the development of a public realm.

The colonial milieu was not a fertile breeding ground for newspapers. In the context of the absolutist rule of the Bourbons, all printed material was subject to censorship, while printing was only allowed through royal privilege. Despite restrictions, a few authorized papers were published in the late eighteenth century in some of the main cities, such as Mexico, Veracruz, Lima, Bogotá, and Buenos Aires, while unauthorized broadsheets, leaflets, and pamphlets also started to circulate in those and other towns, with an increasing presence in the first decade of the nineteenth century. In the case of the licensed press, the initiative came from members of the lettered classes, active in literary and scientific circles, in tertulias and other spaces of elite sociability, and they generally included assorted information that could pass the censors' eyes. Crown officials were attentive to what was published, while in some cases they promoted official chartered papers to publicize government news. In matters of the press, however, Spanish America was way behind most of the Western countries, including Spain.

In this, as in so many other issues, the Cádiz constitution made a difference. In November 1810, it declared freedom of the press, a radical novelty in the kingdom. Despite the reluctance shown by some colonial authorities to enforce this principle, the news of its validation spread fast and, in the context of the political turmoil of those years, "the expansion of printed material became a major force in the conduct of public affairs, broadened 'voice,' and ultimately shaped the outcome of politics."[7]

The revolutionary and immediate postrevolutionary years were particularly prolific press-wise. For the political leadership of all sides, newspapers and more informal printed means of communication became vital tools for the circulation of opinions, ideas, political news and propaganda, proposals for action, appeals to the population, and critical appraisals of rivals and enemies. The governments that came to being in the aftermath of independence all resorted to the creation and circulation of newspapers, while those in the opposition sought to publish their own, with uneven results. Freedom of the press was a most proclaimed principle, but it was frequently overlooked or openly violated, while official censorship and intimidation were sometimes useful mechanisms to silence the voices of the opposition. Periods of strict control were, however, more the exception than the rule, as the government could operate to curtail the influence of the rival press through other means rather than repression. Newspapers that enjoyed official support had many advantages, such as access to financial resources and to relatively efficient circuits of distribution, while the rest had to struggle hard to find both. Thus, even those administrations that were enthusiastic supporters of a free press took advantage of their position to try to prevail among a public that was, during this first half of the century, rather limited. At the same time, political confrontation favored the creation and survival of nonofficial media, so that more often than not, towns and cities throughout Spanish America witnessed a competition among different papers, which were often irregularly published and short-lived.

Whether official or not, the press of this period was a creature of the lettered classes in urban settings, who were also the main consumers of print. But the influence of newspapers was not limited to those who could buy and actually read them. The press was, in the first place, a political arena, and as such appealed to all those involved in partisan struggles; it was, in fact, an instrument of practical politics. Second, reading papers was not always a private, individual, activity. Thus, coffeehouses and reading circles hosted sessions for reading and discussing their contents, while similar encounters took place in taverns and country stores, and even in the street, where literate customers read aloud for the benefit of the illiterate ones. Finally, newspapers were not exclusively political, and they printed information of various sorts (such as news on trade and commerce, on cultural events, on the international situation, among others) that catered for a larger public than the one usually involved in partisan politics. All in all, however, the press of the first half of the century was rather limited in circulation, coverage, and readership, and experienced a very irregular development.

A PASSION FOR NEWSPAPERS

The great and sustained expansion of the press arrived during the second half of the century, when newspapers, dailies, journals, and other printed materials found increasing circulation. "*Por todas partes brotan diarios*": these words printed in 1871 in the Mexican periodical *El Mensajero* are eloquent.[8] A few years earlier, the Argentine *La Tribuna* had already noticed that "there is something extraordinary and marvelous in the rapid development of the press in the last few years."[9] All over Spanish America similar verdicts reflect not only an empirical fact but also an aspiration: the advancement of an institution considered to be "the first instrument of civilization."[10] Carlos Forment counted a total of 1,104 periodicals published in Mexico between 1857 and 1886, most of them created between 1867 and 1881. For Peru, his figures are lower: 211 founded between 1856 and 1875, with a drop in the subsequent years of the War of the Pacific.[11] In Argentina, reliable data refer basically to Buenos Aires. The 1850s witnessed a sudden and sustained printing enthusiasm, after the press restrictions experienced during the Rosas government. The first year after his demise, thirty-two periodicals came to life in the city alone, most of them short-lived. Three decades later, Ernesto Quesada registered 102 newspapers, some of which would prove long-lasting enterprises. By 1887, two of those papers—*La Nación* and *La Prensa*—established in the preceding decades, reached a circulation of eighteen thousand copies each, well above the rest, while the total circulation for all newspapers then published in the city reached one hundred thousand—one copy for every four persons. The figure is quite impressive and compares well with those available for other large contemporary cities.[12]

"Everybody reads the newspapers here . . . from the highest dignitary to the most humble porter."[13] Quesada's perception may be exaggerated, but the number of periodicals in circulation suggests a wide readership. In Buenos Aires, the population that could read and write was on the increase. With ups and downs, literacy rates were also growing in the rest of Spanish America.[14] Thus, the potential public for reading newspapers expanded, although its actual enlargement depended more on the ability of the press to create its own public than on overall literacy figures.

Yet who edited so many newspapers? And for what purposes? Above all, the press was a key piece in the nineteenth-century projects of social and political modernization. In normative terms, as mentioned above, it was considered a fundamental instrument for the development of republican forms of government, as well as for the diffusion of a lettered culture. Its main purpose was not just to represent but rather to forge public opinion. Freedom of the press was tightly connected to this mission, but its actual implementation was a matter of endless public debate. With very few exceptions, the republican governments did not question the right to free speech, but at the same time, there was a widespread concern about the "excesses" of the press. Thus, as Pablo Piccato has pointed out for Mexico, "while the state had to guarantee the freedom of opinion through the press, it also had to build effective institutions to contain the freedom of journalists." And he indicates three main limits: slander, subversion, and immorality as the "basic structure of press restrictions in the nineteenth century."[15] Governments applied them in different ways and following regulations that also varied greatly according to time and place, not just in Mexico but also in the rest of the Spanish American republics. In many of them, and for most of the period, abuses of the press came under the jurisdiction of press juries formed by citizens, which presumably were free from official pressures. Thus, despite the recurrent attempts of governments to control the freedom they proclaimed and were supposed to guarantee, the right to free speech was not seriously or systematically curtailed. Strict censorship was only exceptionally imposed, generally during moments of great political tensions, such as wars and revolutions. The rest of the time, regulations were the rule that allowed a more or less limited but nevertheless sustained relative autonomy of the press.

Newspapers, furthermore, were important political actors. They were the site for the display of political discourse. Political figures and groups used to write for the press, which staged discussions and exchanges among them. Politics became public through these media. The word and even the image (portraits, caricatures) of politicians thus reached different sectors of the population, larger than those usually involved in the partisan game. Each paper, moreover, sought to shape its own community of readers, contributing to forge and to reinforce political identities. Through their actions, newspapers became decisive operators in the political arena.

Thus, the press was a necessary instrument not only for those in power but also for any person, group, or party that sought to have a place in the political life of the republic. Not all of them, however, could afford to edit a paper, an enterprise that required material and cultural resources. Governments usually had their official periodicals, and most political groups either managed to launch and sustain their own, or they sought to establish a close partnership with papers that were not entirely partisan. For decades, official subsidies and subscriptions were the main source of revenue for most newspapers, a fact that hampered their independence and kept them tied to the political networks. At the same time, the craving for printed media opened up opportunities for the creation and development of journalism as a new profession and a risky but eventually rewarding business.

Contemporaries denounced and criticized the "political press" for its formidable power, its mercenary tendency to change sides, and its propensity to magnify debates and disputes. More and more, they argued, it moved away from the enlightened model of public opinion. This critical view is well reflected in the following cunning advice from a character in the Mexican novel *El cuarto poder* to the protagonist who was starting his career in journalism: "Nothing! ... you will not open your mouth without invoking that lady [public opinion], who is a decent person, even though she is in everybody's hands."[16]

The predominance of this type of media, prolific yet dependent upon the disputes and competition among political groups, was very visible around midcentury. It was not, however, the only kind of press in circulation, as important changes were taking place in this variegated field of print and printed materials. In the first place, publications that had different origins and purposes found a fertile ground for development. Commercial, scientific, and literary papers; periodicals created by foreign nationals, by artisans, and by other social, cultural, and ethnic groups; satirical sheets; and other kinds of printed materials increased their circulation in the following decades. Published mainly in the urban areas, they were usually distributed widely within each country. Periodicals were no longer the exclusive terrain of the elites, as the space for public initiative, collective discussion, and group action expanded and gave room to the expression of different interests and opinions. By 1875, the Argentine daily *La Tribuna* pointed out that:

> In Buenos Aires, there is no social or political group that does not have its own press organ. Liberals, reactionaries, pro-government, anarchists, sensible and enlightened people, *tilingos* [snobs], everybody, absolutely everybody, even the foreign residents, have their own periodical to represent their interests.[17]

This quote could easily apply to other places besides Buenos Aires, as editing and printing a paper became a means to participate in public debate no longer monopolized by the lettered few.

Second, the "political" press itself started to change its formats and contents. Although strongly partisan sheets continued to circulate, particularly during electoral periods, the main politicallty oriented papers developed into more complex artifacts. They expanded their contents to include not only the editorials and other politically inspired texts, but other type of news and information articles, both local and international, sections on trade, literary pieces (often in the form of the very popular *folletín*, inspired by the French *feuilleton*), commercial and social ads, and caricatures, among others. Thus, these papers sought to reach a wider public than that of the partisan followers, not only to attract new sympathizers but basically to enlarge their readership. More readers meant more prestige and more sales. In order to expand the autonomous sources of income, editors tried increasing advertisements as well as new methods of distribution and sales, among them street vending.

By the 1860s, therefore, the press was much more diversified and complex than two or three decades earlier. Although short-lived publications of limited circulation proliferated, this was also the era of the great papers, which lasted for decades and reached a wide readership. Such was the case of the Mexican *El Siglo XIX* (1841–96) and *El Monitor Republicano* (1844–96); the Argentine *La Nación* (founded in 1870 and still in circulation), *El Nacional* (1853–93), and *La Tribuna* (1853–84); the Chilean *El Ferrocarril* (1855–1911); and the Peruvian *El Comercio* (founded in 1830 and still in circulation). In between the very ephemeral and the long-lasting periodicals, there was a vast terrain for the expansion of the majority of papers, which succeeded in finding their own public and managed to keep in business for relatively extended periods of time.

During the last quarter of the century, the press went through an even more radical process of change, in tune with developments that had also been taking place in many other parts of the world. The long-lasting relationship between partisan politics and the press weakened, as specialization led to increasing autonomy for both sides. The exaltation of the news as the main purpose of the newspaper, as well as the coming to being of the professional reporter, were key pieces of this transformation. The introduction of up-to-date technologies and working methods turned printing periodicals into a modern business. Readers thus became potential customers in a competitive market where different papers offered their product and services. This transformation, however, took time to come about, and key dailies like *La Nación* in Argentina and *El Imparcial* in Mexico chose to follow the road to modernization, but they did not sever their political connections.

Throughout the century, important changes also took place in relation to the people who made the press. In the first half, newspapers were basically a platform for the men of letters, and most of the main Spanish American writers, publicists, many of them also political figures, were involved in this early journalism. Their presence remained important in the following decades, but new actors came to the fore. The sustained role of the press in politics, the increasing competition among papers to reach an expanding public, and the development of a nonpartisan press opened the way to figures such as the journalist and the professional editor, who gained growing presence in the business of newspapers. Also, the development of technical advancements led to the incorporation of workers with new skills, making the business of publishing more intricate than before. More and diverse kinds of people therefore became involved in this expanding business.

By the end of the century, still more changes would come about: an increasing professionalization (and even the proletarization) of journalists, more sophisticated production techniques, a more efficient organization of the enterprise, a tighter connection with the market, and, finally, the modification of the secular relationship between intellectuals and the press, as the intellectual field gained in autonomy and the press became more professional.

Popular Mobilizations

The press and the associations spoke in the name of public opinion, and contemporaries saw them as the ideal institutions to forge public opinion as well as to represent it. There was a tension, however, between the individual aspiration of each newspaper and association to better achieve that purpose, and the collective dimension of their performance. Indeed, in most of the known cases, the press and the associative movement— as it was called—defined a space of shared initiatives and actions, of dialogue and exchanges, which together sought to embody public opinion. They were, furthermore, not the only actors in the game, as voices and groups that did not fit the model of modern sociability claimed their part.

Public opinion was also the legitimating figure often put forward by men and women who chose to mobilize, to display their physical presence in public spaces in order to express their opinions, to protest, to claim, and to celebrate.[18] Meetings, demonstrations, parades, rallies, marches, pageants, and other collective actions were a familiar spectacle in Spanish American towns and villages. These events could respond to the initiative of very different actors, from governments and the church at the top, to various institutions and organizations, and to more informal groups and sectors of the population who could get together to raise their voices. Scholars have studied this story from very different perspectives that go well beyond the rather limited lens of public opinion used here.

Popular mobilizations have a long and multidimensional history that goes way back to the colonial period, but it was during the republican era that they could claim to embody the actual public and therefore materialize the otherwise rather abstract "public opinion." This identification was particularly relevant in the case of initiatives that came from below; very often, they convened people from different sectors of the population, and even though they might put forward demands originating in specific groups, they sought to appeal to a wider public so as to legitimize a particular claim as one that pertained to "the people" at large. This aspiration responded to the prevailing notion of a unified public opinion, and to the widespread conviction of the virtues of unanimity and the perils of partisanship and social fracture. And although popular mobilizations not always responded to these criteria, during the best part of the century they often followed similar patterns.

Mobilizations were seldom spontaneous, as they required careful preparation and coordination. Different groups and organizations of civil society could convene and lead these gatherings, while the press played a key role in their promotion as well as in their ex post analysis and critique. Political parties also resorted to this type of meeting, and despite their openly partisan bias, they also insisted on their appeal to the general public.

The actual composition and numbers of mobilizations could vary greatly, and so did their motives, specific purposes, and actions. In principle, they were backed by the right of the people to freely assemble, a right that was widely recognized but also strictly regulated, and often suspended or ignored. The perils of tumultuous behavior, violent acts against property and the authorities, and "the excesses of the rabble" led governments to control and repress popular gatherings. At the same time, contemporaries cherished the open manifestation of the people, as an expression of public opinion and commitment, and therefore, wholesale prohibition was out of the question for most of the period. Whether large or small, peaceful or violent, popular mobilizations were a familiar sight in the republican landscape of the nineteenth century, particularly after the midcentury. Governments and politicians had to pay attention to these displays, whether to encourage them as a genuine means of expression of the common interests of the people, to reluctantly accept them as the collective voice of particular groups, or to reject them as false pretenders of public representation. But they could not ignore a practice that had become a regular feature in the complex relationship between government and the people.

The Public(s)

The institutions and practices described so far may be studied as individual cases in the collective organization and action of people from different walks of life. But they were also segments of a larger arena that contributed to shape and give life to the public, that crucial figure of republican politics. Associations and other forms of sociability, as well as the periodical press and other means of printed and oral communication, established actual networks of shared initiatives and exchanges, dialogues and negotiations among themselves and with the political realm. They also defined a more abstract space of shared principles and purposes that positioned them as the incarnation of public opinion.

Scholars have recently understood these developments as symptoms of the formation of a political public sphere. The use of that Habermasian category has helped to account for the shaping of a space of mediation between an increasingly autonomous realm of civil society and the state. At the same time, strictly speaking, this formulation belongs to a much-debated theoretical corpus that has only limited application to our story, so that rather than discussing the advantages and the drawbacks of employing that category, I have followed Pablo Piccato's recent advise of borrowing Habermas's expression and have adopted the notion of public sphere as a "detonator" for our "particular context of research."[19] Most of this chapter responds to the inspiration provided by the many existing discussions on the public sphere in Spanish America, and in what follows, I will resort to that lens to recover some of the points raised in the preceding pages in order to situate my more specific findings within this general framework.

The institutions and practices that claimed to represent the public convened people that came from very different social, ethnic, cultural, and geographical backgrounds and environments. Yet from the early days after independence and throughout most of the century, urban centers were the main loci for these developments, particularly in the case of the newer forms of sociability and the press. Thus, starting around the 1850s, the largest cities, from Mexico to Buenos Aires, to Arequipa, to Lima, to Santiago, and so forth, witnessed an impressive expansion of the means of collective expression and action of different sectors of their population. The actual publics (members of associations, consumers of newspapers, participants in mobilizations) were mainly formed by men and to a lesser extent women, who played minor institutional roles but were a visible presence in this arena. In social and ethnic terms, diversity was the rule for the public at large, while the particular composition of specific publics could be very variable.

Despite the egalitarian creed that guided this world, it was not free from inequalities, discriminations, and exclusions. In most of its institutions, horizontal relationships were cut across by de facto hierarchies that were decisive in securing a tight organization and a smooth performance. These inequalities did not necessarily reflect those of the social world, but the possession of cultural and social capital was an important asset for those aspiring to leadership. Thus, professional men—lawyers, doctors, and such—priests, teachers, artisans, tradesmen, and shopkeepers, were among the most visible heads of these public endeavors.

Most of the population of these republics did not, however, live in the cities, but in rural villages and other country settlements. Collective organization and action followed different criteria than those described above, but the image of a closed world attached to traditional corporate standards does not reflect the complexities of the institutional and communicational changes experienced by most of the communal organizations. Many of the ideas, principles, and forms of action so widespread in urban Spanish America circulated widely in the countryside and contributed to the involvement of the rural areas in the wider picture of a regional or national public sphere. This relationship could spell conflict. Claudio Lomnitz has convincingly argued that, in Mexico, "the creation of a national public sphere, 'fictitious' and highly imperfect though it was, was a real threat for the traditional status of collective actors since it set up an arena where new rules could be made that affected the very acknowledgement of the collectivities in question."[20]

Conceptually, the formation of a political public sphere refers not just to the self-organization of the people but also to the main purpose of such an endeavor: to create an instance of mediation with the state. In most of the Spanish American republics, state formation was, for decades, the project of political elites who understood the development of what we call today a "public sphere" as a necessary aspect of that process. Therefore, they devised means and tried to promote institutions that would contribute to the shaping of national publics. At the same time, actual publics did not necessarily contend to be national, and collective actors often organized and acted at the local and the regional levels. There was, therefore, an intricate pattern of overlapping claims to representation, so that the spatial fragmentation of public spaces did not preclude the existence of an overall instance that assumed a national character.

From a normative point of view, the institutions and practices of the public sphere are defined as spaces ruled by the laws of reason, where dialogue among equals prevails within, while peaceful exchanges and negotiations are the main tools for putting forward claims and demands to the state and the political realm. These ideals had wide acceptance in our nineteenth-century republics, and there were practical and rhetorical efforts to prove their worth in the actual functioning of publics. Quite often, however, aggressive impositions, belligerent actions, or otherwise violent displays became effective tools of public performance. On these occasions, the theoretically solid frontiers between the usually antagonistically driven political sphere and the allegedly more "civilized" and ordered public realm crumbled. Such recurring experiences did not do away with the widespread conviction that there was a fundamental difference between the two—the former corrupt, the latter virtuous.

A second opposition enhanced this difference, that which pitted the divisive nature of partisan politics versus the unanimity of the public sphere. For most of the century, fear of the fracture of the body politic led to a widespread preference for a unitary notion of the common good, prevalent in the political languages in circulation. In this context, while partisan politics remained a strongly criticized but apparently inevitable feature of the life of the republics, the realm of public opinion and action embodied unity. In the face of divisions of, and conflicts among, the actual publics, each part claimed to represent the whole and to act in the name of the people at large. Thus, although often contested in practice, unanimity was seldom challenged in principle. Only by the last decades of the century, the question of plurality came to the fore, of the legitimacy of putting forward particular claims in the public realm, and of the contours of the common good.

References

Adelman, Jeremy. 2006. *Sovereignty and Revolution in the Iberian Atlantic.* Princeton, NJ: Princeton University Press.

Agulhon, Maurice, Bernardino Bravo Lira, et al. 1992. *Formas de sociabilidad en Chile, 1840–1940.* Santiago: Fundación Mario Góngora.

Alonso, Paula. 2003. *Construcciones impresas: Panfletos, diarios y revistas en la formación de los estados nacionales en América Latina, 1820–1920.* Buenos Aires: FCE.

Altamirano, Carlos, dir. 2008. *Historia de los intelectuales en América Latina.* Vol. 1, *La ciudad letrada: De la conquista al modernismo,* by Jorge Myers. Buenos Aires: Katz.

Baker, Keith. 1987. "Politics and Public Opinion under the Old Regime: Some Reflections." In Censer and Popkin, *Press and Politics.*

———. 1990. *Inventing the French Revolution.* Cambridge: Cambridge University Press.

Banti, Alberto M., and Marco Meriggi, eds. 1991. "Élites e associazioni nell'Italia dell'ottocento." *Quaderni Storici* 77 (2).

Bedoya, María Elena. 2010. *Prensa y espacio público en Quito, 1792–1840.* Quito: FONSAL.

Bourdieu, Pierre. 1980. "L'opinion publique n'existe pas." In *Questions de Sociologie.* Paris: Les éditions de Minuit.

Calhoun, Craig. 1992. *Habermas and the Public Sphere.* Cambridge, MA: MIT Press.

Canal y Morell, Jordi. 1993. "El concepto de sociabilidad en la historiografía contemporánea (Francia, Italia y España)." *Siglo XIX: Revista de Historia,* n.s., 13 (January–June).

Castro, Miguel Ángel, and Guadalupe Curiel, eds. 2003. *Publicaciones periódicas mexicanas del siglo XIX: 1856-1876 (Parte I).* Mexico City: Universidad Nacional Autónoma de México.

Castro-Klarén, Sara, and John Charles Chasteen, eds. 2003. *Beyond Imagined*

Communities: Reading and Writing the Nation in Nineteenth-Century Latin America. Baltimore: Johns Hopkins University Press.

Censer, Jack R., and Jeremy D. Popkin, eds. 1987. *Press and Politics in Pre-Revolutionary France*. Berkeley: University of California Press.

Chambers, Sarah. 2003. "Letters and Salons: Women Reading and Writing the Nation." In Castro-Klarén and Chasteen, *Beyond Imagined Communities*.

Chamosa, Oscar. 2003. "'To Honor the Ashes of Their Forebears': The Rise and Crisis of the African Nations in the Post-Independence State of Buenos Aires, 1820–1860." *The Americas* 59 (3).

Charney, Evan. 1998. "Political Liberalism, Deliberative Democracy, and the Public Sphere." *American Political Science Review* 92 (1).

Chartier, Roger. 1995. *Espacio público, crítica y desacralización en el siglo XVIII: Los orígenes culturales de la Revolución Francesa*. Barcelona: Gedisa.

Cibotti, Ema. 1988. "Mutualismo y política, un estudio de caso: La Sociedad Unione e Benevolenza en Buenos Aires entre 1858 y 1865." In *L'Italia nella società argentina*, edited by Fernando Devoto and Gianfausto Rosoli. Rome: Centro Studi Emigrazione.

———. 1994. "Periodismo político y política periodística: La construcción de una opinión italiana en el Buenos Aires finisecular." *Entrepasados* 6.

Clark de Lara, Belem, and Elisa Speckman Guerra, eds. 2005. *La república de las letras: Asomos a la cultura escrita del México decimonónico*. 3 vols. Mexico City: Universidad Nacional Autónoma de México.

Cruz Soto, Rosalba. 2005. "Los periódicos del primer período de vida independiente (1821–1836)." In Clark de Lara and Speckman Guerra, *La república de las letras*, vol. 2.

Cucchi, Laura. 2013. "Opinión pública, legitimidad y partidos: Miradas sobre el adversario político en Córdoba a finales de los años setenta del siglo XIX." *Boletín del Instituto de Historia Argentina y Americana "Dr. Emilio Ravignani"* 38.

———. 2014. "Prensa política y legislación de imprenta en Córdoba en la segunda mitad del siglo XIX." *Revista de Indias* 74 (260).

Cucchi, Laura, and María José Navajas. 2012. "Un actor 'incómodo': Prensa política en Córdoba y Tucumán a fines de la década de 1870; Discursos, prácticas y representaciones." *Secuencia: Revista de Historia y Ciencias Sociales* 82.

Del Aguila Peralta, Alicia. 1997. *Callejones y mansiones: Espacios de opinión pública y redes sociales y políticas en la Lima del 900*. Lima: Pontificia Universidad Católica del Perú.

Del Castillo Troncoso, Alberto. 2005. "El surgimiento de la prensa moderna en México." In Clark de Lara and Speckman Guerra, *La república de las letras*, vol. 2.

Del Palacio Montiel, Celia. 2006. "Redes de información y circulación de impresos en México: La prensa de Guadalajara en las primeras décadas del siglo XIX." *Revista Iberoamericana* 214 (January–March).

Del Palacio Montiel, Celia, comp. 2000. *Historia de la prensa en Iberoamérica*. Mexico City: Altexto.

Di Stefano, Roberto, Hilda Sabato, Luis Alberto Romero, and José Luis Moreno. 2002. *De las cofradías a las organizaciones de la sociedad civil: Historia de la iniciativa asociativa en Argentina, 1776–1990*. Buenos Aires: GADIS.

Escalante Gonzalbo, Fernando. 1992. *Ciudadanos imaginarios*. Mexico City: El Colegio de México.

Falcón, Romana. 2006. "El arte de la petición: Rituales de obediencia y negociación, México, segunda mitad del siglo XIX." *Hispanic American Historical Review* 86 (August).

Fraser, Nancy. 1990. "Rethinking the Public Sphere: A Contribution to the Critique of the Actually Existing Democracy." *Social Text* 25/26.

Forment, Carlos. 2003. *Democracy in Latin America, 1760–1900*. Chicago: University of Chicago Press.

Frega, Ana, and Mónica Maronna. 2016. "La opinión pública como espacio de disputa." In *América Latina: De la independencia a la crisis del liberalismo, 1810–1930*, edited by Nuria Tabanera and Marta Bonaudo. Madrid: Marcial Pons; Zaragoza: Prensas de la Universidad de Zaragoza.

Gantús, Fausta. 2009. *Caricatura y poder político: Crítica, censura y represión en la ciudad de México, 1876–1888*. Mexico City: El Colegio de México/Instituto de Investigaciones Dr. José María Luis Mora.

García Bryce, Iñigo. 2004. *Crafting the Republic: Lima's Artisans and Nation Building in Peru, 1821–1879*. Albuquerque: University of New Mexico Press.

Gazmuri, Cristián. 1992. *El "48" chileno: Igualitarios, reformistas, radicales, masones y bomberos*. Santiago: Editorial Universitaria.

Goldman, Noemí. 2000. "Libertad de imprenta, opinión pública y debate constitucional en el Río de la Plata (1810–1827)." *Prismas: Revista de historia intelectual* 4.

González Bernaldo de Quirós, Pilar. 1993. "Las pulperías de Buenos Aires: Historia de una expresión de sociabilidad popular." *Siglo XIX: Revista de Historia*, n.s., 13 (January–June).

———. 1999a. *Civilité et politique aux origins de la nation Argentine: Les sociabilités à Buenos Aires, 1829–1862*. Paris: Publications de la Sorbonne.

———. 1999b. "Literatura injuriosa y opinión pública en Santiago de Chile durante la primera mitad del siglo XIX." *Estudios Públicos* 76.

———. 2004. "La 'sociabilidad' y la historia política." In Pani and Salmerón, *Conceptualizar lo que se ve*.

Grez Tosso, Sergio. 1993. "The Mutual Benefit Movement in Chile from Its Origins to the Present Times (1853–1992)." *International Social Security Review* 46 (3).

Guedea, Virginia. 2005. "Las publicaciones periódicas durante el proceso de independencia (1808–1821)." In Clark de Lara and Speckman Guerra, *La república de las letras*, vol. 2.

Guerra, François-Xavier. 1992. *Modernidad e independencias: Ensayos sobre las revoluciones hispánicas*. Madrid: MAPFRE.

———. 2003. "Forms of Communication, Political Spaces, and Cultural Identities in the Creation of Spanish American Nations." In Castro-Klarén and Chasteen, *Beyond Imagined Communities*.

Guerra, François-Xavier, Annick Lempérière, et al. 1998. *Los espacios públicos en Iberoamérica: Ambigüedades y problemas, Siglos XVIII–XIX*. Mexico City: FCE.

Gunn, J.A.W. 1983. *Beyond Liberty and Property: The Process of Self-Recognition in Eighteenth-Century Political Thought*. Montreal: McGill-Queen's University Press.

Gutiérrez Sanín, Francisco. 1995. *Curso y discurso del movimiento plebeyo, 1849–1854*. Bogotá: Instituto de Estudios Políticos y Relaciones Internacionales/El Ancora ediciones.

Habermas, Jürgen. 1965. *Strukturwandel der Öffentlichkeit*. Berlin: Luchterhand.

———. 1990. "Philosophy as Stand-In and Interpreter." In *Moral Consciousness and Communicative Action*, by Jürgen Habermas and Christian Lehnardt. Cambridge, MA: MIT Press.

Halperin Donghi, Tulio. 1985. *José Hernández y sus mundos*. Buenos Aires: Sudamericana.

Hoffmann, Stefan-Ludwig. 2003. "Democracy and Associations in the Long Nineteenth Century: Toward a Transnational Perspective." *Journal of Modern History* 75 (June).

Illades, Carlos. 1996. *Hacia la república del trabajo: La organización artesanal en la ciudad de México, 1853–1876*. Mexico City: El Colegio de México.

Jacobsen, Nils. 2005. "Public Opinions and Public Spheres in Late-Nineteenth-Century Peru: A Multicolored Web in a Tattered Cloth." In *Political Cultures in the Andes, 1750–1950*, edited by Nils Jacobsen and Cristóbal Aljovín de Losada. Durham, NC: Duke University Press.

Jaksić, Iván, ed. 2002. *The Political Power of the Word: Press and Oratory in Nineteenth-Century Latin America*. London: Institute of Latin American Studies.

Keane, John. 1998. *Civil Society: Old Images, New Visions*. Cambridge: Polity Press.

Koselleck, Reinhart. 1972. *Kritik und Krise: Eine Studie zur Pathogenese der bürgerlichen Welt*. Frankfurt-am-Main: Surhkamp.

Landes, Joan B. 1988. *Women and the Public Sphere in the Age of the French Revolution*. Ithaca, NY: Cornell University Press.

Lomnitz, Claudio. 1995. "Ritual, Rumor, and Corruption in the Constitution of Polity in Modern Mexico." *Journal of Latin American Anthropology* 1 (1).

McEvoy, Carmen. 1997. *La utopía republicana: Ideales y realidades en la formación de la cultura política peruana (1871–1919)*. Lima: Pontificia Universidad Católica del Perú.

Monsiváis, Carlos. 2005. "Del saber compartido en la ciudad indiferente: De grupos y ateneos en el siglo XIX." In Clark de Lara and Speckman Guerra, *La república de las letras*, vol. 1.

Mücke, Ulrich. 2004. *Political Culture in Nineteenth-Century Peru: The Rise of the Partido Civil*. Pittsburgh: University of Pittsburgh Press.

Myers, Jorge. 1995. *Orden y virtud: El discurso republicano en el régimen rosista*. Bernal: Universidad Nacional de Quilmes.

———. 1999. "Una revolución en las costumbres: Las nuevas formas de sociabilidad de la elite porteña, 1800–1860." In *Historia de la vida privada en la Argentina*. Vol. 1, edited by Fernando Devoto and Marta Madero. Buenos Aires: Taurus.

Nord, Philip. 1995. *The Republican Moment: Struggles for Democracy in Nineteenth-Century France*. Cambridge, MA: Harvard University Press.

Ozouf, Mona. 1988. "'Public Opinion' at the End of the Old Regime." *Journal of Modern History* 60 suppl. (September).

Palti, Elías. 2003. "La Sociedad Filarmónica del Pito: Opera, prensa y política en la República Restaurada (México, 1867–1876)." *Historia Mexicana* 52 (4).

———. 2004. "Guerra y Habermas: Ilusiones y realidad de la esfera pública latinoamericana." In Pani and Salmerón, *Conceptualizar lo que se ve*.

———. 2005a. *La invención de una legitimidad: Razón y retórica en el pensamiento mexicano del siglo XIX (Un estudio sobre las formas del discurso político)*. Mexico City: Fondo de Cultura Económica.

———. 2005b. "La transformación del liberalismo mexicano en el siglo XIX: Del modelo jurídico de la opinión pública al modelo estratégico de la sociedad civil." In Sacristán and Piccato, *Actores, espacios y debates*.

———. 2008. "Tres etapas de la prensa política mexicana del siglo XIX: El publicista y los orígenes del intelectual moderno." In Altamirano, *Historia de los intelectuales*.

Pani, Erika. 2005. "'Para difundir doctrinas ortodoxas y vindicarlas de los errores dominantes: Los periódicos católicos y conservadores en el siglo XIX." In Clark de Lara and Speckman Guerra, *La república de las letras*, vol. 2.

Pani, Erika, and Alicia Salmerón, eds. 2004. *Conceptualizar lo que se ve: François-Xavier Guerra, historiador, Homenaje*. Mexico City: Instituto Mora.

Pérez Rayón, Nora. 2005. "La prensa liberal en la segunda mitad del siglo XIX." In Clark de Lara and Speckman Guerra, *La república de las letras*, vol. 2.

Piccato, Pablo. 2005. "Honor y opinión pública: La moral de los periodistas durante el porfiriato temprano." In Sacristán and Piccato, *Actores, espacios y debates*.

———. 2010. "Public Sphere in Latin America: A Map of the Historiography." *Social History* 35 (2).

Pinedo Soto, Adriana, and Celia del Palacio Montiel. 2003. *Prensa decimonónica en México*. Morelia:Universidad Michoacana; Guadalajara: Universidad de Guadalajara.

Poblete, Juan. 2003. *Literatura chilena del siglo XIX: Entre públicos lectores y figuras autoriales*. Santiago: Editorial Cuarto Propio.

————. 2006. "La revista, el periódico y sus lectores en el chile decimonónico." *Revista Iberoamericana* 214 (January–March).

Quesada, Ernesto. 1883. "El periodismo argentino (1877–1883). *Nueva Revista de Buenos Aires*, year 2, vol. 9.

Rabasa, Emilio. 1949. *El Cuarto Poder y Moneda Falsa*. Mexico City: Editorial Porrúa.

Ramos, Julio. 2003. *Desencuentros de la modernidad en América Latina*. Mexico City: Fondo de Cultura Económica. 1st ed., 1989.

Reina, Leticia. 1997. *La reindianización de América, siglo XIX*. Mexico City: Siglo XXI/CIESAS.

Robertson, Andrew W. 1995. *The Language of Democracy: Political Rhetoric in the United States and Britain*. Charlottesville: University of Virginia Press.

Rojas, Rafael. 2003. *La escritura de la Independencia: El surgimiento de la opinión pública en México*. Mexico City: Taurus/CIDE.

Rojkind, Inés. 2012. " 'El gobierno de la calle': Diarios, movilizaciones y política en Buenos Aires del novecientos." *Secuencia: Revista de Historia y Ciencias Sociales* 84 (September–December).

Romero, Luis Alberto. 1997. *¿Qué hacer con los pobres? Elite y sectores populares en Santiago de Chile, 1840–1895*. Buenos Aires: Sudamericana.

Rubio Correa, Marcial. 2003. *La constitucionalización de los derechos en el Perú del siglo XIX*. Lima: Pontificia Universidad Católica del Perú.

Ryan, Mary. 1997. *Civic Wars: Democracy and Public Life in the American City during the Nineteenth Century*. Berkeley: University of California Press.

Sabato, Hilda. 1998. *La política en las calles: Entre el voto y la movilización; Buenos Aires, 1862–1880*. Buenos Aires: Sudamericana. In English: *The Many and the Few: Political Participation in Republican Buenos Aires*. Stanford, CA: Stanford University Press, 2001.

————. 2001. "On Political Citizenship in Nineteenth-Century Latin America." *American Historical Review* 106 (4).

————. 2002. "Estado y sociedad civil, 1862–1920." In Di Stefano, Sabato, Romero, and Moreno, *De las cofradías a las organizaciones de la sociedad civil*.

————. 2008. "Nuevos espacios de formación y actuación intelectual: Prensa, asociaciones, esfera pública (1850–1900)." In Altamirano, *Historia de los intelectuales*.

Sabato, Hilda, ed. 1999. *Ciudadanía política y formación de las naciones: Perspectivas históricas de América Latina*. Mexico City: Fideicomiso de Historia de las Américas de El Colegio de México/Fondo de Cultura Económica.

Sabato, Hilda, and Ema Cibotti. 1990. "Hacer política en Buenos Aires: Los italianos en la escena pública porteña, 1850–1880." *Boletín del Instituto de Historia Argentina y Americana, Dr. Emilio Ravignani*, 3rd series, 2.

Sabato, Hilda, and Alberto Lettieri, comps. 2003. *La vida política en la Argentina del siglo XIX: Armas, votos y voces*. Buenos Aires: Fondo de Cultura Económica.

Sacristán, Cristina, and Pablo Piccato, eds. 2005. *Actores, espacios y debates en la historia de la esfera pública en la ciudad de México*. Mexico City: Instituto de Investigaciones Históricas de la UNAM/Instituto de Investigaciones Dr. José María Luis Mora.

Sanders, James E. 2014. *The Vanguard of the Atlantic World: Creating Modernity, Nation, and Democracy in Nineteenth-Century Latin America*. Durham, NC: Duke University Press.

Serrano, Sol. 2008. *¿Qué hacer con Dios en la República? Política y secularización en Chile (1845–1885)*. Santiago: Fondo de Cultura Económica.

Sociedad Tipográfica Bonaerense. 1862. *Memoria de la Comisión Directiva*.

Strum, Arthur. 1994. "A Bibliography of the Concept of Öffentlichkeit." *New German Critique* 61.

Suárez de la Torre, Laura. 2004. "Monumentos de tinta y papel: Batallas por la modernidad; El mundo editorial de la primera mitad del siglo XIX." In Pani and Salmerón, *Conceptualizar lo que se ve*.

Taylor, Charles. 1990. "Modes of Civil Society." *Public Culture* 3 (1).

Uribe-Uran, Victor M. 2000. "The Birth of a Public Sphere in Latin America during the Age of Revolution." *Comparative Studies in Society and History* 42 (2).

———. 2006. "The Great Transformation of Law and Legal Culture: 'The Public' and 'the Private' in the Transition from Empire to Nation in Mexico, Colombia, and Brazil, 1750–1850." In *Empire to Nation: Historical Perspectives on the Making of the Modern World*, edited by Joseph W. Esherick, Hasan Kayali, and Eric Van Young. Lanham, MD: Rowman and Littlefield.

Vázquez Semadeni, María Eugenia. 2010. *La formación de una cultura política republicana: El debate público sobre la masonería. México, 1821–1830*. Mexico City: Universidad Nacional Autónoma de México.

Warner, Michael. 1990. *The Letters of the Republic: Publication and the Public Sphere in Eighteenth-Century America*. Cambridge, MA: Harvard University Press.

———. 2005. *Publics and Counterpublics*. New York: Zone Books.

Warren, Richard A. 2001. *Vagrants and Citizens: Politics and the Masses in Mexico City from Colony to Republic*. Lanham, MD: SR Books.

CHAPTER FIVE

The Republican Experiment

AN ESSAY IN INTERPRETATION

AFTER THE SEVERANCE of the colonial links with Spain, the adoption of republican forms of government based on the principle of popular sovereignty brought about important changes in the ways of defining and legitimating political power and authority in the American territories of the former empire, and inaugurated a decades' long history of political experimentation. The introduction of representative government entailed the definition and redefinition of the actual role of the sovereign people, of the relationships between that people and government, and of the boundaries of inclusion in and exclusion from the polity. The exploration of three dimensions of political life as it developed in the new republics in the making, I have argued, may throw some light on how those relationships and boundaries were defined and changed over time. Across Spanish America, throughout the nineteenth century, elections, armed citizenship, and public opinion became pillars in the construction and legitimization of authority. The norms, institutions, and practices associated with them were central to play the game of power, and although they were not the only pieces in that game, they referred to a crucial aspect of the republican regimes: political power involved not just the elites and would-be elites, it implicated larger sectors of the population in significant forms of organization and action.

To compete for and reach office, whether by peaceful or violent means, the few had to resort to the many. That political formula remained constant throughout the nineteenth century, although both its terms and the relationship between them were always changing. By exploring the main spheres that materialized that relationship, we have illuminated how each of them worked and who were the political actors involved. This chapter will, in turn, propose to articulate these partial pictures into an overall interpretation of the republican experiment in Spanish America. It will first address the question of the political actors—who were the few and the many of our story—and then move to the engine of the political life of the period: the dynamics of competition and conflict.

"The Ruling Few"[1]

Historian Tulio Halperin Donghi coined the revealing term "career of the revolution" to refer to the opportunities for "public service" and "individual advancement" opened during and after the transition from colony to republic for men of personal and political ambitions. In a groundbreaking study centered on the former Viceroyalty of the River Plate, he traced the steps that led to the formation of a new political leadership in the aftermath of the revolution of 1810.[2] In the midst of the uncertainties and innovations of that period, political life broke its former limits that, albeit always in flux, had served to keep struggles for power restricted within the parameters imposed by imperial rule. The collapse of the colonial order, the ensuing wars, and the new political frameworks for the definition of authority undermined the grounds upon which colonial authorities reigned, while economic and social elites at large were also subject to the convulsions of the day. In that context, the dismantling and reconstruction of political order was not a straightforward event but, rather, an intricate and conflicting process in which, Halperin Donghi convincingly argues, new leaderships took shape. In this regard, there was a deep break with the colonial era, and despite connections and continuities with the imperial past, the revolution brought about decisive innovations in the realm of politics and a wide renewal of political personnel, not just for the River Plate but for the whole of Spanish America.[3]

By the 1820s, the men who had managed to rise to a position of leadership struggled to acquire, keep, and reproduce political power, while others tried to enter the game. The former were a variegated lot with different personal and political stories and trajectories, but most of them had fought the material and symbolic wars that culminated with independence. From then on, the initial choice for republican forms of government provided a broad framework within which the leadership conducted the normative debates on the organization of the polity, shaped its institutional edifice, and headed practical political action. Their daily options in this regard would further mold political life in each of the republics, in ways that generally proved to be quite dynamic. By focusing upon elections, armed citizenship and the militia, and public opinion, we have seen how the norms, institutions, and practices changed throughout the century and affected the definition and exercise of citizenship. They also had important consequences for the leadership, and together with other dimensions of politics, they contributed to some long-term trends in the shaping of the "few."[4]

The turbulence of revolutions and wars brought about both a renewal and an enlargement of the leadership: new and more men were attracted to politics. They came from different social and cultural backgrounds, well beyond the circles that had nurtured the colonial elites. The abolition of the caste system, the nobility titles, and the qualifications related to *limpieza de sangre* (racial purity) meant that the formal stratifications of the Old Regime were left behind. Social and cultural differences, however, did not disappear, and despite the widespread proclamation of the principle of equality, hierarchies of various sorts continued to prevail during the whole century. An ingrained and long-lasting partition distinguished *gente decente* or *gente de bien* and *plebe*, but as the century advanced, this two-tiered system lost its descriptive and value-charged effectiveness. The social structure was reshaped, as new and different social groups defined the pyramidal representation of a modern society.

In politics, however, social stratifications did not necessarily carry force. At a time of great social and political commotions, like the one experienced by Spanish America at the beginning of the nineteenth century, the established links between those spheres easily fall apart. In this case, the combined effects of the crumbling of the old order, the circulation of new values, and the opportunities that arose for the creation of fresh leadership opened the way to a greater autonomy of the political sphere vis-à-vis the social realm. Elaborate and changing relations connected both spheres of human action, but the political was in no way automatically subordinated to the social, and the internal hierarchies of the former cannot be subsumed in those of the latter.

The postrevolutionary leaderships came mostly from the ranks of the *gente decente* widely considered—a social category whose borders were in flux. The possession of some property and education plus the peers' recognition of an honorable way of life remained relevant features to qualify. Race played a role but the former proscription of *castas* (mixed bloods) was effectively abolished, and in fact, quite a few of the top political leaders qualified as *mestizos* and *mulatos*.[5]

To enter politics a certain amount of social and cultural capital helped, but wealth, connections, and education alone did not make a leader. Opportunities arose from the material extension and functional complexities of the newly created political networks, for those men who could deploy the resources and abilities needed to carry out the tasks demanded by republican politics—such as command troops and win wars, coordinate and mobilize electors, court and direct public opinion, and so on. This scenario demanded an increasing specialization for those devoted to politics—regardless of how they made a living. They could be *rentiers* and members of wealthy families that provided for their material needs, but more often than not they were originally practicing lawyers (the main profession among politicians), priests (particularly important in the aftermath of independence), teachers, publicists, merchants, hacendados, government employees, and professional military, among other occupations considered "honorable" by contemporaries.

The presence of numerous generals, commanders, brigadiers, captains, and colonels is often seen as a symptom of the presumably dominant role of the military in Spanish American politics. Yet for most of the nineteenth century, those titles resulted from the widespread involvement of men coming from different professions and occupations in armed conflicts where they received their ranks. Few of them, however, were career officers. The formation of professional armies with strict discipline, established hierarchies, and internal solidarities came late in the century, so that most of the so-called military did not belong to a specific, self-identified, corporate group. As we have already mentioned, access to and command of armed resources was a decisive asset for aspiring political leaders, but these did not need to be professionals to succeed in that enterprise.

Decentralization was another relevant factor in the constitution of leaderships. Different causes favored this tendency. The collapse of the colonial territorial organization produced a dismemberment of sorts, where localities of different size and former status claimed to recover and retain their sovereign powers. Political life resurfaced and took shape at that level, and for a long time, resisted the attempts on the part of centralizers to rein it in. Later in the century, the strengthening of national scenarios did not put an end to the more restricted ones, particularly as regards political practices. Thus, for example, electoral and militia networks, as we have seen, had strong local and regional groundings. This overall situation opened opportunities for men from the provinces or from municipalities far away from the centers of economic and cultural power, who could thus join the ranks of the political leadership.

The ascent of regional caudillos fits this picture: they were men who proved capable of mounting powerful political machines—involving military force, electoral potential, and personal charisma—at the local level and eventually connect to larger networks of power. In the existing literature on Latin American politics, the figure of "caudillo" has occupied center stage, associated with the militarization of the revolutionary era and its aftermath.[6] The image of the unruly warlord who exerted command and influence upon his retinue and imposed his arbitrary rule over a specific area under his control started to circulate already in the nineteenth century. During the struggles of the postrevolutionary decades, contemporaries applied the term to criticize such leaders as Facundo Quiroga, in the River Plate; Manuel Belzú in Bolivia; José Antonio Páez, in Venezuela, or José Gervasio Artigas, in Uruguay, among many others, for their presumably uncivilized style of leadership, based on personal power, military might, and no regard for institutions. After the wars, which had bred *caudillismo*, Spanish America could not supersede this type of rule and, in contrast to more politically stable areas of the Western world, where civilian leadership was the norm, it remained caught in this refractory, antimodern system.

Later scholars recovered this nineteenth-century view, and, in conceptualizing *caudillismo*, they mostly retained—with few variations—the basic features put forward by contemporaries. In recent years, historians have questioned different aspects of that conventional interpretation, particularly in regard to its presumably archaic nature. Rather, they have reinserted caudillos in the complex webs of political transformations brought about—precisely—by the transition to modernity. The long years of war empowered certain figures that succeeded in mobilizing men for the armies and in gaining their support and following. They could put this capital to good use in the struggles for power characteristic of the decades of nation-building, but in that new context, military might and personal charisma were not enough. Continued success in politics meant that they entered into the more elaborate networks of republican life, which included norms, institutions, and practices at the local level but also connections with the rest.

Caudillos had to be politicians, but not all politicians were caudillos. As the century advanced, the word lost its specificity and was applied largely to strong personal leaderships, usually with negative connotations. Also, the fabric of politics showed increasing complexity, and required new skills and resources different from those that caudillos had mastered in the past. Decentralization remained, however, a long-lasting trait of nineteenth-century political life, particularly at the level of practices, but national articulation became more and more important and, although those aspiring to positions of high leadership generally started their careers locally, they could only get to the top once they reached a national standing.

Within this context of renewal, expansion, and decentralization of political leaderships, the "few" were, in fact, not so few, but recruitment was far from being universal. More so than the existing legal restrictions to occupy government posts, it was the nonexplicit sociocultural frontiers that limited the access to the ranks of leader politicians. Politics demanded resources and connections not available to all citizens. The borders were porous and variable, but perceptible to all. At the same time, below those men at the top, the new political structures included a large number of intermediaries, successive links in the chain that connected the main figures with the rank and file. At these levels, recruitment went well beyond the social limits of the *gente decente* to include men from the wide plebeian world, and later in the century—when this initial division waned—from the increasingly differentiated middling sectors of society. These social differences, however, were not necessarily replicated in the political realm, which had its own internal stratification.

Thus, politicians became almost a class in themselves, with their own hierarchies and protocols. They had connections to the social and economically powerful, and often entered into the same social circles, but they were not their natural offspring or their unconditional pawns. In tune with republican traditions, those at the top prided themselves to be an aristocracy of sorts, an elite, not on account of material wealth or hereditary status but rather, on their merits and virtues as "best men" of the nation. Their power came from different sources, not least among them, those that derived from their ability to appeal to the many.

The Sovereign People

Since the early days of the nineteenth century, in Spanish America the sovereign people was considered the ultimate source of political authority. It was an abstraction that evoked, at the same time, the unitary character of the principle of sovereignty and the plurality of individuals voluntarily come together through the *pactum societatis*. In the process that led to the formation of the new polities, this abstraction materialized into the actual people who became an indispensable presence in the political landscape. From then on, individuals living within a particular political community enjoyed certain rights considered "natural" and therefore "universal," while at the same time not all of them were entitled to the other set of rights that were more specific—among them, political rights. The definition of who enjoyed what, that is, of the extent and limits of citizenship in its various forms, was a matter of continual debates and disputes within each polity. That was the case with political and civil liberties in Spanish America, as the new republics established the conditions of citizenship, and thus demarcated the theoretical limits of the universe of the significant "many."

In all of Spanish America, the criteria for the definition of citizenship and its boundaries followed a similar course throughout most of the century, with few exceptions and local variations. The enthusiastic adoption of that institution in the aftermath of the revolutionary era aimed at shaping a polity based upon the equality of its members, thus putting an end to the strongly stratified colonial social order. Citizenship introduced, however, new differences among the people, according to their rights and obligations. In the early days of the republics, these were widely extended among the male population, so that a majority of the free, nondependent, adult men were formally citizens. But there were also many who did not enter into this category, as we have seen in chapter 2. From then on, this initial demarcation experienced changes, toward both contraction and expansion, but throughout the best part of the nineteenth century, the normative boundaries of political citizenship remained relatively broad for males—that is, compared to most European countries and even some areas of the United States—while civil liberties were widely recognized, albeit subject to the ups and downs of political fluctuations.

In principle, legal frameworks entitled individuals to exercise their rights and take part in the political life of the republic; among them, those related to the three dimensions described in former chapters: elections, armed citizenship, and public opinion. As we have seen, citizenship opened the way for the inclusion of most adult men into the militia and electoral networks, while civil liberties entitled many more—including women and dependent males, as well as nonnationals—to engage in the public sphere. Actual participation shows that the people made use of their rights in various degrees and forms. Thus, patterns of involvement differed across time and space, as well as according to other factors, including age, gender, social and cultural backgrounds, and place of residence. A very broad overview points to the strong representation of young adult men from the popular classes—both urban and rural—among voters and militiamen, while a wider spectrum took part in other instances of electoral events as well as in the encouragement and material support of the militia's displays and actions. The people joining what we now call the "public sphere" were even more varied, with a visible commitment of the urban middling sectors and the literate, but also with the presence of women, children, slaves, and others not formally considered as citizens.

It is misleading, however, to focus on individuals, classified according to demographic and occupational attributes. In practice, political involvement was mainly channeled through collective mechanisms of participation, both formal and informal, and therefore, it is to those mechanisms that we should turn to observe politically engaged citizens in action.

Representative forms of government required that those who aspired to reach power win elections, and remain under the control of the people via armed citizenship and public opinion. These were the three main established forms of relationship between the many and the few, and although they were not the only means for the people to raise their voices or display their action in public, nor the only mechanisms for politicians to amass power, they remained indispensable parts of the political life of Spanish American republics throughout the nineteenth century.

Competition for power on the part of the few required the attraction, recruitment, organization, and deployment of followers and sympathizers. Electoral and militia networks had a relevant role in this regard and, I have argued, these did not result from the spontaneous initiative of individual citizens but, rather, they were the outcome of the sustained work of politicians of different levels, from the top leaders down to the local brokers. Despite their many differences, most of these networks were stratified structures where the rank and file occupied the lower levels. Therefore, they were at the same time highly inclusive and strongly hierarchical organizations, where asymmetric relationships and exchanges prevailed. This verticality should not lead us to presume, however, that those who participated were just cannon fodder in the disputes among the powerful. Examples abound to show that, in most of the known cases, members responded to different motivations and incentives, while subordination seldom implied subservience. Their commitment to a leader, a local boss, or a party depended upon many factors, among which coercion played mostly a minor role. As we have seen, there were material and symbolic retributions for those joining in a partisan network, which in many ways also operated as an instance of protection and belonging. Ideological affinities and shared sensibilities, extended family and friendship ties, and the actual experience of political action often cemented the links among the membership. Asymmetry did not preclude agency, and those at the bottom of the pyramid could and did use their place to negotiate and claim, as well as to put their own views and opinions in circulation, both individually and collectively. Within this very general framework, there were many differences among regions and periods, from the strongly patriarchal and deferential patterns that prevailed, for example, in the rural areas of Chile to more porous and flexible relationships found in other settings, such as parts of Mexico and Colombia during the liberal years after the midcentury, among other possible arrangements.[7]

The wide range of institutions and practices related to public opinion offers a rather different picture from the one just portrayed for electoral and militia networks. Uniform patterns of organization are harder to find among the participants of traditional and new associations, the newspaper publics, and the many types of mobilizations that claimed to embody and represent public opinion. By the middle of the century, the people involved were probably more numerous and diverse; their participation more autonomous; their bonds looser and maybe more egalitarian, although not free from hierarchies and discriminations. At the same time, these webs stemming from civil society partially overlapped with partisan networks, and although contemporaries—and later scholars—portrayed the former as the virtuous opposite of the latter, more often than not they were tightly intertwined in the complex fabric of republican politics.

Altogether, then, polities founded upon the principle of an equal people generated spaces of political involvement that were at the same time inclusive and stratified, that is, unequal. The formal (and informal) incorporation of large sectors of the population to the political life of most Spanish American republics did not equate with the establishment of an egalitarian polity. Republican political practices created and reproduced inequalities, not because they were devised to exclude (as scholars frequently have argued) but rather because inclusion took place in strongly hierarchical contexts of participation. Thus, egalitarian norms did not materialize in egalitarian institutions or practices. The introduction of popular sovereignty and the principle of political equality was a key revolutionary gesture aiming at the erosion of the strongly stratified world typical of colonial society. But the incoming order generated its own political hierarchies, which differed from the previous ones, as well as from the new and changing patterns of social stratification. Indeed, the vertical components found in the electoral, military, and civic networks did not replicate those of the social structure—although they could partially overlap— rather, they resulted from the political dynamics, its practices and institutions.

At the same time, social belonging (class), ethnicity, and gender played their part in the novel hierarchies inasmuch as those dimensions were embedded in the normative frameworks and within the actual political practices. Thus, gender distinctions were explicit: women were formally excluded from the vote and the militia and had a relatively marginal role in the public sphere. Men from the laboring classes, in turn, were included but for the most part subordinated to a leadership that, though recruited from a relatively ample social spectrum, predominantly came from the better-off. Ethnic considerations were as good as erased from the norms, but they partially lived on in everyday life. There was a high correlation, moreover, between social class and race, and although not all "Indians" and particularly not all mestizos or mulattoes were lower class, most of the indigenous groups were peasants, while the majority of Afro-Americans belonged to the laboring sectors. Even if the borders between class and race were porous, and involvement in politics could help men move across the social and ethnic divide, there were limits to such mobility, which was usually not disruptive enough to change the dominant patterns of social reproduction. Questions regarding these limits, as well as the ways in which class, ethnicity, and gender connect to political hierarchies, therefore, require further exploration.

These patterns of participation were not incompatible with the republican order; on the contrary, they were their creatures. In this context, tensions arising from the asymmetry between equality of rights and the inequalities resulting from the exercise of those rights were sometimes the cause of political disputes.[8] More often than not, however, these tensions did not get in the way of the legitimacy of the system. Nor was the predominance of collective forms of participation that left little room for individual autonomous involvement a cause for serious contestation, at least until the last quarter of the century when, as we shall see, this whole dynamic came under heavy criticism.

Partisan Networks

The involvement of the people in the political life of the Spanish American republics was not limited to the institutions and practices just described. These were, however, the main channels for the participation of the many in the struggles for power that punctuated the history of the nineteenth century. The numbers of those involved fluctuated greatly. In practical terms, the political networks set up to compete for power featured a variable number of men and to a lesser degree women from very different status and backgrounds engaged in collective forms of action. Political practices, therefore, cut across the social, ethnic, and cultural divides and shaped shared spaces of identification and belonging.

The fact that these mechanisms functioned along hierarchical lines led some scholars to dismiss their relevance for the majority of the people, particularly for the lower classes, and to read them as devises basically instrumental to the elites. In the last decades, historians attuned to the perspectives put forward by subaltern history and other versions of a "history from below" have proposed a very different and richer picture. They portray the "subaltern" participating actively in politics by advancing their own agenda. Whether in the context of the disputes among the elites, or by launching their own, autonomous actions, different popular groups contested the order imposed from above and fought to transform it. In this view, social and cultural cleavages find their way to the political arena; political identity is tightly tied to class and ethnicity, and the nineteenth century is seen as one more stage in the long-living struggle between the subaltern and the powerful. This perspective has brought to light important aspects of the political life of the Spanish American republics, such as the ample repertoire of popular collective actions that aimed at eroding and resisting the existing social order. Subaltern agency did not preclude subalterns' participation in formal politics, and some of the best recent studies in this line of work explore their role within the liberal parties in Mexico, Peru, and Colombia during the second half of the nineteenth century. The emphasis lies, however, on the autonomy of the subalterns within the frameworks defined by elite politics, and on their capacity to define and put forward their own collective targets, always different from and usually opposed to those of their elite occasional partners.

The insistence upon the autonomy of the subaltern and their axiomatic opposition to the elites or the powerful, however, leaves aside a large part of the story of republican politics in Spanish America, which featured people from very different social and ethnic backgrounds joining in partisan networks that operated under shared political banners. Their participation raises the question of their commitment to parties and leaders. Why should we presume that the subaltern in those groups followed, by definition, their own collective agenda guided by their struggle against the established order? Why not ask if, alongside their respective social and cultural identities, they developed political attachments with their fellow partisans of different backgrounds? Members of an electoral club, a militia regiment, a civic association, and other similar bodies could develop strong links as a result of their shared political and public experiences, besides their respective social and cultural attachments. Party allegiance, loyalty to one or another caudillo, sustained support for a leader, fidelity toward a group, all merit close examination in each specific case, as political identities did not necessarily equate with social or ethnic belonging.

There are many examples that show subalterns (or plebeians) actively involved in political activity in very different sides of the political and the ideological spectrum, from conservatives to liberals, from federalists to centralists, and so forth, as well as among the following and supporters of competing leaders or circles within these larger constellations. Scholars have sometimes interpreted this fact as a symptom of the instrumental character of that involvement: subalterns took part in whatever side responded to their collective demands, regardless of their position in the partisan game the elites played. Yet it can also be an indication of actual commitment of individuals and groups originating in the popular classes to different parties and leaders through various forms of involvement, which could indeed include negotiation of collective interests but also affinity with ideas and programs; loyalty or deference to caciques, caudillos, and party bosses; bonds of shared political experience, and so forth. Case studies that explore the connections of specific social and ethnic groups to the institutions and practices of republican politics show a variety of situations in this regard, from the elaborate arrangements that connected some indigenous groups to republican politics to the more conventional deferential relations in rural societies to the relatively more open interactions typical of urban spaces.

As for those who participated actively in political networks but belonged to the *gente de bien* or *gente decente*, they also developed partisan attachments that did not necessarily correlate with their class background. Partisan politics was a dividing factor among the socioeconomic elites, as well as among the lower echelons of the well-to-do and the middling sectors of the social scale. Specific material interests could have an important place in defining party allegiances, but so did ideas, traditions, personal affinities, and partisan identities as well as fears and expectations. So, it is not exceptional to find members of the same family adhering to different parties, and even fighting on opposite sides in wars and revolutions.

Political leaders stemmed mainly from those sectors, and it was the fracture among them that fueled most of the struggles for power in nineteenth-century Spanish America. Actions from below—such as collective demands for land, rebellions against taxes, litigations in courts of law, petitions to the authorities, or other public displays—could sometimes challenge the powerful, but competition to reach and control overall positions of authority was basically conducted from above and featured partisan networks that vertically incorporated men and women from the rest of the social spectrum. These organized forms of political intervention did not develop into stable structures but remained, rather, flexible arrangements that brought together locally grounded leaders (of different levels) who could recruit and mobilize followers and sympathizers to participate in the political disputes of the day. This pattern changed gradually, and by the midcentury, political alignments showed signs of growing stability and territorial articulation. Quite often, as described in chapter 2, different regional and local partisan outfits converged within the loose framework of a few larger national political organizations increasingly known as "parties." These lacked the type of institutional buildup and legitimacy that came to define later-day parties and remained as rather flexible and variable networks of men and resources operating under a single umbrella in the political arena. They often featured as familiar actors in the public instances such as parliament and the press, thus creating collective forms of identification that transcended the local sphere. A few decades later, new developments led to a deep reassessment of the role of parties. From then on, as formally organized institutions, they became the accepted and desired mechanisms of association and the preferred means to channel opinions and interests within the political system. In this context, each party established internal rules and procedures,

THE REPUBLICAN EXPERIMENT [187]

regulated membership, and developed novel forms of recruitment and participation as well as tighter mechanisms of
control, which inaugurated a new era in the ways of partisan
involvement.

Competition and Conflict

Nineteenth-century Spanish American political life spelled
conflict. In this regard, the new republics faced dilemmas that
were similar to those confronted by previous experiences, such
as the early republican United States as well as postrevolutionary France. A normative ideal of unanimity prevailed, which
understood politics as an instance of production and expression of the common good that would guard these republics
from the threats of divisionism and disbandment. Differences
of opinion were presumably sorted out through rational debate
that elucidated the collective will. From the very beginning,
however, sheer competition for power among different groups
set in and conflict followed, while existing institutional mechanisms were not prepared to channel that sort of antagonism.
For several decades, contemporaries stuck to the founding
principles, condemned partisan discord, and tried to bridge
the gap between normative ideals and actual practices through
constant experimentation—as we have seen throughout this
book. Political rivalries, in turn, found many ways of expression, and resulted in recurrent confrontations, as contending
forces resorted to all recognized means available, both formal
and informal, in order to win.

Scholars have long discussed the causes of political antagonism among the few—ranging from very general and enduring
issues, such as the ideological divide between conservatives
and liberals or the divergences between centralists and federalists, to more circumstantial matters that fueled most of the

actual conflicts of the day. Regardless of the final reasons that may or may not explain why men with similar relatively privileged social and cultural backgrounds became political enemies, the fact is that their rivalries animated a dynamic, often turbulent, political life. During the best part of the century, governments were usually ephemeral, leaderships contested, territorial boundaries uncertain, and political regimes subject to successive changes. With few exceptions, the hegemonic projects that were successively tried in most republics failed, and those that succeeded experienced recurrent challenges to their rule. This political instability proved long lasting and raised persistent concern among nineteenth-century thinkers and publicists. Later scholars have in turn recovered that topic as part of a diagnosis that sees the turbulences of the era as failures specific to Latin American politics. Their respective frameworks, however, are very different.

At the time, contemporaries contrasted their experience with the ideal of the republic as a virtuous form of government and political organization and found it lacking. Actual competition for power and sustained antagonism among political actors ran counter to the paradigm of a unified polity. Different means were proposed to avoid "factionalism" as well as to manage partisan conflicts. Results remained controversial. Contemporaries were critical of solutions that did not match their republican values—such as restrictions to voting or to the autonomy of the militia—while at the same time they discussed those same principles and searched for new ways to curb instability and tame politics.

Twentieth-century scholars followed a different line of argument. They contrasted the virulence of nineteenth-century politics with the concept of "order" that came to prevail at the end of that century—as we shall see—and that still endures as a measuring rod to critically evaluate the period under study.

In this case, political "order" is associated with a predictable institutional regime with clear and undisputed rules for the legitimization and exercise of authority. Seen under this light, most of the nineteenth-century Spanish American republics were a failure, the result of an incomplete or defective political modernization.

At this point, I would like to propose a somewhat different interpretation of these experiences. Rather than flawed examples within the larger picture of modern republics, they may be read as deeply embedded in that tradition. Between the 1820s and the 1870s, the Spanish American republican political order was strongly shaped by a civic rhetoric that favored the *vita activa* of the members of the polity, a shared ideal that presided over the foundation of these regimes. Despite the founders' critical appraisal of the human resources available for their political venture, they put forward a relatively inclusive definition of male citizenship, which—together with the imperatives of war—resulted in a wide-ranging mobilization of different sectors of the population. For decades, this initial definition was reproduced with scarce variation as part of a political dynamic marked by the struggles for power among different political groups headed by the few but actively engaging the many. Partisan competition led to the organization and display of electoral forces, "citizens in arms," and popular demonstrations of different sorts, as well as to sharp rhetorical exchanges in the press, the legislative bodies, and other public arenas. Rituals, words, and symbols played their part in extolling civic involvement and in defying adversaries and enemies, while political action reinforced and renewed the vertical and horizontal bonds between those participating in partisan confrontations.

At a time when the centralization of state power was a highly contested proposition, political life was—with few exceptions—highly decentralized. Local and regional leaderships struggled to keep political power in their hands, a modus operandi that conspired against any attempt at creating an overall hegemonic instance of domination. The fragmentation of military forces—the double-tiered system of a standing army and militia with strong local roots—was at the heart of that system, and its persistence was strongly upheld by important segments of the ruling elites as well as by wider sectors of the population. This institutional and political pattern resulted in recurrent instability, which was not the outcome of the failure to play the game of the republic, but on the contrary, a result of a specific way of abiding by its rules.

Overall, the system was quite successful in creating and delivering legal authority, but the same principles and mechanisms that served to bestow legitimacy upon institutions and practices could also be deployed to challenge the results of their application. In the name of the "people," contemporaries contested elections and staged revolutions. With the adoption of the principle of popular sovereignty to found authority, transcendence was left behind, and once power came to be considered a human construct, uncertainty slipped in. The invention of the people sought to replace the divine right of kings, but the people were not above human intervention, and therefore, authority claims could easily be contested. Also, the norms and institutions were, themselves, subject to criticism, and to proposals for change, making them always precarious.

Uncertainty and instability were not exclusive to the Spanish American world. Republican experiences in late eighteenth- and nineteenth-century Europe offer several examples of the difficulties in establishing and reproducing legitimate authority within those kinds of regimes. In most cases, like those of France and later Italy and Spain, among others, republics proved short-lived and were replaced by other systems.

The United States, the most successful case, was not free from the same type of challenges, which were met by repeated institutional and political innovations that enabled the relatively peaceful processing of partisan antagonism. These, however, were insufficient to solve the deepest conflict of all, which cut the republic in two, triggered a long and bloody civil war, and was over only after one of the rival sides defeated the other in the battlefields. Important reforms to the republican regime followed this outcome and resulted in the consolidation of stable political order.

Spanish Americans, in turn, insisted on the initial basic patterns for fifty years, and although they also tried different ways to tame politics, it was only by the last decades of the century that they decidedly opted out of some of the former practices and embraced the tenets of a new order.

The Rules of the Game

During the core decades of the republican era, the unstable and unruly features of politics raised concerns among the ruling sectors, who were, at the same time, the architects and main beneficiaries of the existing political order. The initial revolutionary enthusiasm of the 1810s had encouraged the first steps toward the dismantling of the highly stratified colonial system and the creation of a more egalitarian basis for the new polities, while the necessities of war favored the mobilization of vast sectors of the people and their incorporation to armies, guerrillas, and their rear guard. After independence, the efforts to establish a new, republican, order triggered intense ideological debates as well as fierce political disputes. Already in the late 1820s and early 1830s, publicists and political leaders were alarmed by the turbulences of politics, which they attributed to different causes, from colonial heritage to the nonvirtuous behavior of elites or to the unruly behavior of the populace.

Among the favorite normative measures to "civilize" politics were the introduction of restrictions to citizenship, through limitations to the suffrage (see chapter 2), the reduction or dismantling of militias (see chapter 3), and the censorship of the press (see chapter 4). More drastic solutions, however, were also tried, such as the concentration of all authority in the hands of a strong figure, very much in the classical tradition of republican dictators but also in the more local recent manner of caudillos. Others, in turn, advocated a return to some sort of corporate arrangement reminiscent of the Spanish colonial past. These were, of course, ideal models that never quite materialized, but figures such as Juan Manuel de Rosas in Buenos Aires and Gaspar Rodríguez de Francia in Paraguay, among others, may be associated with republican dictators, while early conservatives in Mexico and Colombia sought to reestablish a corporate order. Very few of these experiments of the first half of the century managed to curb political instability for more than a relatively short time. As this book has clearly shown, strong restrictions to citizenship rights and practices had limited effects, while most dictatorial and corporate regimes were frequently disturbed by political contestation.[9]

Around the midcentury, fresh ideas and proposals circulated in Spanish America, mostly introduced and sustained by self-defined "liberals" of various sorts, but which soon appealed to other sectors across the social as well as the political spectrum. In this new climate, several republics redefined their institutional organization following the tenets of constitutional liberalism and set up new rules, which confirmed the original republican values and practices, and at the same time sought to establish limitations to the exercise of government power.[10] The constitutions sanctioned in Argentina and Colombia in

1853, Mexico in 1857, Ecuador in 1861, Venezuela in 1864, all respond to this pattern. In that context, the abolition of slavery,[11] the end to Indian *tributo* (head tax),[12] the relative expansion of the suffrage, and a specific advocacy of civil liberties and the separation of powers prevailed. The disentailment of communal lands, belonging to the church or to indigenous peoples, was a highly controversial issue that was only partially enforced. This measure aimed mainly at dismantling all remnants of a corporate social order by reinforcing the individual right to private property. At the same time, it was part of a larger objective, that of limiting the social, economic, cultural, and political power of the Catholic Church—a contested proposition that aroused many passions. All these changes gave new vigor to political life, which experienced the relative enlargement of citizenship and popular mobilization, a development of the public means of collective action, and an expansion of armed resources.

In terms of the institutional organization, the new charters also established the rules for the definition and exercise of authority at the national level and its articulation with local powers, in designs that ranged from the federal model inspired by the United States to the centralized arrangements that found an important precedent in the Chilean constitution of 1833. These reforms succeeded in creating the basic institutions of a national administration as well as in regulating the relationships between the legislative, judicial, and executive powers.

In this new context, however, instability remained a prevailing feature in the political life of most republics. The persistence of rivalries that were played out in different scenarios continued to animate a brisk, often violent, display of competing forces. Liberals came to power in several places, but they were usually internally fragmented and also challenged by other political groups, particularly conservatives of various sorts. In practical terms, partisan competition continued to rely upon the organized mobilization of men coming mainly from the popular classes under the aegis of deeply divided leaderships. The already established forms of political participation were partially modified, but the basic dynamics of confrontation persisted. More consistently than before, elections were the main road to public office; they were held regularly and frequently, convened a relatively limited but increasing number of voters, and gathered many more people around demonstrations of partisan force. The improvement of controls over procedures reduced arbitrariness at the polls, but they did not succeed in eradicating the use of force. At the same time, the development of electoral clubs and other forms of political association turned electoral conjunctures from one-time events into extended occasions for the display of partisan rhetoric, rituals, and actions. Newspapers produced and amplified political messages, together with the reproduction of images of candidates and public figures. They were part of a public sphere that gained increasing relevance after the midcentury and contributed to the repercussion of partisan disputes among a larger audience. Thus, for example, in the turbulent year of 1873 in Buenos Aires, the daily *La Tribuna* underscored the widespread appeal of partisan politics among the urban population:

> The young women today are annoyed by the light literature of the gossip columns. . . . They would rather read a large article on politics. . . . The same thing happens with kids at school. . . . The bootblacks and street urchins talk about electoral combinations. . . . A young man cannot visit a family without the girls of the house or their mother demanding he profess his political faith.[13]

Involvement in the public sphere or participation in public spaces through the periodical press, civic associations, street demonstrations, and other collective forms of expression ani-mated a vibrant civic life, particularly in the cities. Most of these practices related to the concerns of different sectors of civil society that put forward their own agendas, not void from political definitions but allegedly free from partisan interven-tion. In times of turbulence, however, the borders between these spheres of action blurred, so that their ordinary mutual connections intensified and left little room for autonomy.

Revolutions were some such occasions. From the 1850s to the 1870s, as we have seen, armed uprisings against the estab-lished authorities were frequent in most of the Spanish Ameri-can republics. Efforts at institutionalization did not preclude the continuation of this form of political action, based on the traditional argument of the right and obligation to defend free-dom in the face of despotism. Contested elections, with accusa-tions of factionalism and fraud, remained a frequent cause for rebellion. Despite rising criticism that pointed to the material and human costs of *levantamientos*, these were enthusiasti-cally advocated not only by sectors of the partisan leadership but also by many of their followers. The material bases for this practice, moreover, remained strong. These decades saw the affirmation of militia in the shape of the National Guard in most of these countries, as the expression of the principle of armed citizenship and, in the case of federal polities, as a means of enhancing state or provincial powers. The fragmen-tation of the armed forces—particularly the coexistence of mi-litia and standing armies but also their territorial partitions—facilitated the access to military resources, indispensable to launch a revolution. This period was ripe with them, thus con-tributing to the recurrent instability of political regimes.

At the same time, the 1860s witnessed the first systematic attempts to curb military fragmentation in the context of con-flicts that required a drastic modernization of the armies. War on a new scale resulted from the French intervention and subsequent civil war in Mexico (1862–67), the Spanish occupation of the Chincha Islands in 1864–66, which was defeated by Peruvian and Chilean forces (supported also by Bolivia and Ecuador), and the bloodiest confrontation of them all, between 1864/65 and 1871, which involved Paraguay on one side and Argentina, Brazil, and Uruguay on the other. At the end of the 1870s another large war broke out, this time pitting Chile against Peru and Bolivia. These conflicts were of a different magnitude than the usual internal struggles. The countries involved, therefore, soon had to face the fact of their military flaws, as well as the crude realities of large-scale violence. Divided forces, which lacked a central command and a coordinated leadership, could hardly meet the new challenges.

In the context of these wars, therefore, overall military organization was subject to practical changes. Standing armies acquired increasing importance, as governments made huge efforts to modernize them in terms of equipment, training, and hierarchical structure. Thus, they started to operate with greater efficiency than before, while militia forces were subordinated to their command and experienced increasing difficulties to sustain their autonomy. These changes did not amount to an overall eradication of the dual military system, but rather to recurrent debates and political disputes around these issues, as well as to discussions regarding the different alternatives. In fact, it was not until the following decades that in the context of wider changes in the relationships between politics and society, the coexistence of standing army and militia gave way to the predominance of the former and the dismantling of the latter. In the meantime, the militia continued to be a significant institution in the complex relationships between the many and the few that materialized popular sovereignty.

In short, the variations introduced after the midcentury in the norms and institutions of the republics added complexity to their political life, but they did not alter the basic patterns of the political practices that had prevailed since the 1820s for the exercise of citizenship and the legitimization of authority.

Fin de Siècle

By the 1870s, concerns regarding political instability grew stronger, and from then on, the whole edifice of the republican experiment described in this book came under heavy fire, both in the realm of ideas and in the empirical world of practices. In the last decades of the century, the Spanish American societies experienced important transformations at all levels.

Most countries were going through a relatively sustained process of economic expansion as they developed closer links with the world markets, while the social structure became more diversified and complex. New ideas circulated challenging old certainties. Among them, those put forward by positivism in its different versions were strongly influential. Politics, in turn, was at the center of an overall revision of the values and practices that had founded and shaped the republics. Political languages changed. A rising creed put forward a concept of order that favored stability and discipline, rather than the active mobilization typical of elections and revolutions of old. The advocates of that order attributed instability mainly to the fragmentation of authority as well as to the "factionalism" of a divided leadership and its reliance on a popular following with unruly or unpredictable behavior. They strove, therefore, to centralize authority in a strong national state that would monopolize the use of force, discipline the elites, and reshape the citizenry. Once they reached positions of power, they pushed forward policies that went in those directions, and were often in consonance with the newly prevailing trends among sectors of the leadership and beyond.

Thus, as described in chapter 2, in some countries the right of suffrage was restricted, while in others those in power sought to strengthen controls from above. New ways of understanding politics favored the representation of different interests and opinions in the political realm, so that some sort of proportional mechanisms replaced the winner-take-all former system while parties now became a genuine and desired means of channeling the people's voice and vote. Competition among them was now considered legitimate, thus diminishing the tensions of electoral confrontation. This new type of party, furthermore, operated as a formal institution that introduced regulations to supervise both the leaders and the rank and file, and while it opened the door to a wider recruitment of followers than its predecessors, it also tightened the mechanisms for managing their actions.

Another pillar of the former model, the citizen in arms, became practically extinct. Militias and national guards were either eliminated or put under the control of increasingly centralized standing armies. The dual system that had produced and reproduced the fragmentation of the armed forces was dismantled, as military power concentrated in the professional armies, which featured as a decisive instrument of the national state (chapter 3). Revolutions, in turn, lost much of their former appeal, not only because of changes in the conceptual framework that had considered them legitimate but also on account of the mounting difficulties to gain access to military resources. Finally, the symbolic and ritual facets of armed citizenship that associated it with republican patriotic virtues withered away in the face of a new sort of national patriotism that correlated with the army and the citizen soldier now recruited mainly through conscription.

Changes also happened in the public realm in tune with the transformations experienced by an increasingly multifaceted civil society and by a more sophisticated state apparatus. Publics multiplied, and their connections to politics followed different patterns with more variations than before, while efforts on the part of governments to control or discipline their voices and actions usually had limited success.

The transformation of these forms of popular participation in politics and of the institutions and practices that channeled the relationship between the many and the few were part of larger epochal political changes in the ways of the republic. These changes did not go unchallenged, as new social and political forces soon contested the incoming model. Their proposals and demands, however, were only marginally voiced in republican terms; rather, critics of the new system found arguments in socialist ideals and democratic theories to put forward their claims. The languages of class, interest, and race displaced the civic rhetoric that had prevailed in previous decades, while national identity discourse permeated republican patriotism and new forms of political action buried the old. These fin de siècle overall trends present in most of the Spanish American republics did not affect them evenly; rather, they opened diverging ways for the following century.

References

This chapter relies on a vast bibliography, most of which has already been mentioned in previous chapters. This selection therefore includes only works not already listed as well as those specifically mentioned in the text of the chapter.

Alda Mejías, Sonia. 2002. *La participación indígena en la construcción de la república de Guatemala, s. XIX*. Madrid: UAM ediciones.

Andrews, George Reid. 2007. *Afro-Latinoamérica, 1800–2000*. Madrid: Iberoamericana, Frankfurt am Main. Vervuert.

Alonso, Paula, and Beatriz Bragoni, eds. 2015. *El sistema federal argentino: Debates y coyunturas (1860–1910)*. Buenos Aires: Edhasa.

Appelbaum, Nancy, Anne S. Macpherson, and Karin Alejandra Rosemblatt, eds. 2003. *Race and Nation in Modern Latin America*. Chapel Hill: University of North Carolina Press.

Birle, Peter, Wilhelm Hofmeister, Guenther Maihold, and Barbara Potthast, comps. 2007. *Elites en América Latina*. Frankfurt am Main: Vervuert; Madrid: Iberoamericana.

Botana, Natalio. 1984. *La tradición republicana: Alberdi, Sarmiento y las ideas políticas de su tiempo*. Buenos Aires: Sudamericana.

Caplan, Karen D. 2010. *Indigenous Citizens: Local Liberalism in Early National Oaxaca and Yucatán*. Stanford, CA: Stanford University Press.

Carmagnani, Marcello, ed. 1993. *Federalismos latinoamericanos: México/Brasil/Argentina*. Mexico City: Fondo de Cultura Económica.

Carvalho, José Murilo de. 1990. *A formação das almas: O imaginário da república no Brasil*. São Paulo: Companhia das Letras.

———. 1995. *Desenvolvimiento de la ciudadanía en Brasil*. Mexico City: Fideicomiso de Historia de las Américas de El Colegio de Mexico/Fondo de Cultura Económica.

Chaves de Mello, Maria Tereza. 2007. *A república consentida: Cultura democrática e científica do final do Império*. Rio de Janeiro: Editora FGV/Edur.

Deas, Malcolm. 1993. *Del poder y la gramática y otros ensayos sobre historia, política y literatura colombianas*. Bogotá: Tercer Mundo editores.

De Jong, Ingrid, and Antonio Escobar Ohmstede, eds. 2016. *Las poblaciones indígenas en la conformación de las naciones y los Estados en la América Latina decimonónica*. Mexico City: El Colegio de Mexico/CIESAS; Zamora, Michoacán: El Colegio de Michoacán.

Doyle, Don, ed. 2017. *American Civil Wars: The United States, Latin America, Europe, and the Crisis of the 1860s*. Chapel Hill: University of North Carolina Press.

Drake, Paul. 2009. *Between Tyranny and Anarchy; A History of Democracy in Latin America, 1800–2006*. Stanford, CA: Stanford University Press.

Falcón, Romana. 2006. "El arte de la petición: Rituales de obediencia y negociación, México, segunda mitad del siglo XIX." *Hispanic American Historical Review* 86 (August).

Goldman, Noemí, and Ricardo Salvatore, comps. 1998. *Caudillismos rioplatenses: Nuevas miradas a un viejo problema*. Buenos Aires: Eudeba.

Greene, Jack P., and Philip D. Morgan, eds. 2009. *Atlantic History: A Critical Appraisal*. New York: Oxford University Press.

Guardino, Peter. 1995. "Barbarism or Republican Law? Guerrero's Peasants and National Politics, 1820–1846." *Hispanic American Historical Review* 75 (2).

———. 1996. *Peasants, Politics, and the Formation of Mexico's National State: Guerrero, 1800–1857*. Stanford, CA: Stanford University Press.

———. 2005. *The Time of Liberty: Popular Political Culture in Oaxaca, 1750–1850*. Durham, NC: Duke University Press.

Guerra, François-Xavier. 1988. *México del Antiguo Régimen a la Revolución*. Mexico City: Fondo de Cultura Económica.

Gutiérrez, Francisco. 1995. *Curso y discurso del movimiento plebeyo, 1849/1854*. Bogotá: El Ancora Editores.

Halperin Donghi, Tulio. 1972. *Revolución y guerra: Formación de una elite dirigente en la Argentina criolla*. Buenos Aires: Siglo XXI.

———. 1986. *Historia contemporánea de América Latina*. Madrid: Alianza editorial.

Irurozqui, Marta, ed. 2005. *La mirada esquiva: Reflexiones históricas sobre la interacción del estado y la ciudadanía en los Andes (Bolivia, Ecuador y Perú), siglo XIX*. Madrid: Consejo Superior de Investigaciones Científicas.

Jaksić, Iván, and Eduardo Posada Carbó, eds. 2011. *Liberalismo y poder: Latinoamérica en el siglo XIX*. Santiago: Fondo de Cultura Económica.

Joseph, Gilbert M., ed. 2001. *Reclaiming the Political in Latin American History: Essays from the North*. Durham, NC: Duke University Press.

Joseph, Gilbert M., and Daniel Nugent, eds. 1994. *Everyday Forms of State Formation: Revolution and Negotiation of Rule in Modern Mexico*. Durham, NC: Duke University Press.

Lynch, John. 1992. *Caudillos in Spanish America, 1800–1850*. Oxford: Clarendon Press.

Mallon, Florencia. 1995. *Peasant and Nation: The Making of Postcolonial Mexico and Peru*. Berkeley: University of California Press.

Méndez, Cecilia. 2005. *The Plebeian Republic: The Huanta Rebellion and the Making of the Peruvian State, 1820–1850*. Durham, NC: Duke University Press.

———. 2006. "Las paradojas del autoritarismo: Ejército, campesinado y etnicidad en el Perú; siglos XIX al XXI." *Íconos: Revista de Ciencias Sociales*, no. 26 (Quito).

Morelli, Federica, Clément Thibaud, and Geneviève Verdo. 2009. *Les empires atlantiques des Lumières au libéralisme (1763–1865)*. Rennes: Presses Universitaires de Rennes.

Palacios, Guillermo, ed. 2007. *Ensayos sobre la nueva historia política de América Latina, siglo XIX*. Mexico City: El Colegio de Mexico.

Peart, Daniel, and Adam I. P. Smith, eds. 2015. *Practicing Democracy: Popular Politics in the United States from the Constitution to the Civil War*. Charlottesville: University of Virginia Press.

Posada Carbó, Eduardo, ed. 1998. *In Search of a New Order: Essays on Politics and Society in Nineteenth-Century Latin America*. London: ILAS.

Riekenberg, Michael. 2014. *Staatsferne Gewalt: Eine Geschichte Lateinamerikas (1500–1930)*. Frankfurt: Campus Verlag.

Rock, David. 2002. *State Building and Political Movements in Argentina, 1860–1916*. Stanford, CA: Stanford University Press.

Sabato, Hilda. 2001. *The Many and the Few: Political Participation in Republican Buenos Aires*. Stanford, CA: Stanford University Press.

———. 2006. "La reacción de América: La construcción de las repúblicas en el siglo XIX." In *Europa, América y el mundo: Tiempos históricos*, edited by Roger Chartier and Antonio Feros. Madrid: Marcial Pons.

———. 2017. "Arms and Republican Politics in Spanish America: The Critical 1860s." In Doyle, *American Civil Wars*.

Servín, Elisa, Leticia Reina, and John Tutino, eds. 2007. *Cycles of Conflict, Centuries of Change: Crisis, Reform, and Revolution in Mexico*. Durham, NC: Duke University Press.

Stein, Stanley J., and Barbara H. Stein. 1970. *The Colonial Heritage of Latin America: Essays on Economic Dependency in Perspective*. New York: Oxford University Press.

Tabanera, Nuria, and Marta Bonaudo, eds. 2016. *América Latina: De la independencia a la crisis del liberalismo, 1810–1930*. Madrid: Marcial Pons; Zaragoza: Prensas de la Universidad de Zaragoza.

Thomson, Guy. 1990. "Bulwarks of Patriotic Liberalism: The National Guard, Philharmonic Corps, and Patriotic Juntas in Mexico, 1847–88." *Journal of Latin American Studies* 22 (1).

———. 1998. "Order through Insurrection: The Rise of the District of Tetela during Mexico's Liberal Revolution, 1854–1876." In Posada Carbó, *In Search of a New Order*.

———. 2010. "¿Convivencia o conflicto? Guerra, etnia y nación en el México del siglo XIX." In *Nación, Constitución y Reforma, 1821–1908*, edited by Erika Pani. Mexico City: CIDE/Fondo de Cultura Económica.

Thomson, Guy, with David LaFrance. 1999. *Patriotism, Politics, and Popular Liberalism in Nineteenth-Century Mexico: Juan Francisco Lucas and the Puebla Sierra*. Wilmington, DE: Scholarly Resources.

Thurner, Mark. 1997. *From Two Republics to One Divided: Contradictions of Postcolonial Nationmaking in Andean Peru*. Durham, NC: Duke University Press.

Thurner, Mark, and Andrés Guerrero, eds. 2003. *After Spanish Rule: Postcolonial Predicaments of the Americas*. Durham, NC: Duke University Press.

Vázquez, Josefina Zoraida. 2009. *Dos décadas de desilusiones: En busca de una fórmula adecuada de gobierno (1832–1854)*. Mexico City: El Colegio de México/Instituto Mora.

Wood, James. 2011. *The Society of Equality: Popular Republicanism and Democracy in Santiago de Chile, 1818–1851*. Albuquerque: University of New Mexico Press.

Epilogue

FOR MOST OF the nineteenth century the Americas were a republican continent. After the severance of the colonial bonds, almost all of the newly formed independent states became republics, from the United States in the north to Chile and Argentina in the Southern Cone, and kept that form of government for good.[1] This experience was quite unique, as during that period, other systems prevailed around the globe. The Atlantic revolutions had challenged absolutism and succeeded in introducing new principles for the institution of society and the foundation of political authority. The sovereignty of the people replaced the divine right of kings in several European countries and opened the way to what we now call "political modernity" on both sides of the Atlantic. But this change did not go uncontested, and for many decades to come, absolutist rule prevailed in large parts of the world.

The Americas went the way of the new and became a vast testing field in the institution of forms of "living in common" attuned to the novel values. The United States had taken a bold step when it chose the form of government and, rather than following the British road to modernity via a constitutional monarchy, it opted for the republic. This was a risky move, with few precedents in modern times. Revolutionary France soon followed, but only for a short period, as the political convulsions of the 1790s heralded the demise of the republic, and the establishment of Napoleon's imperial regime. When the time came for self-rule in Spanish America, the prevalent international trend was promonarchy, but that option was politically defeated there, and sooner rather than later the new polities endorsed the republican alternative.

Republics and constitutional monarchies came in many forms. Both systems displaced transcendence and understood the political as a human construct, but there was a fundamental difference between the two. In the face of the uncertainties generated by the lack of an ultimate—divine—reference for power, typical of the modern polity, the monarchy functioned as a unifying principle for the community and the monarch as the symbolic head of the realm that provided an anchor for the new order. The hereditary rule, moreover, offered an invariable and predictable mechanism for succession, while royal lineage embodied tradition and continuity with the collective past.[2] Republics, in turn, had no such moorings; the people were the first and the last instance in the institution of the polity and in the foundation of authority—and what they decided to build they could agree to dismantle. This fundamental conundrum was at the heart of the construction of republics, whose architects devised different institutional and practical means to instill certainty and stability into the new political order.

In this book, I have argued that the actual nineteenth-century republican regimes had different ways of facing the challenges posed by this common dilemma. Some of them, like the first and second French republics, did not manage to survive for long. Others, like the Spanish American ones, succeeded in time by experimenting with a diversity of norms, institutions, and practices throughout the century, in a sequence that was characteristically unstable. The United States, in turn, was a unique case of a highly original republic, which from its early days devised a series of political innovations that steered the regime in a relatively stable, long-term course with few—albeit critical—exceptions.

The story told in these pages helps illuminate the larger picture of political modernity around the world. It has focused on the making of the Spanish American republics in the postcolonial era when the territories that had been for over three centuries under imperial rule severed their colonial bond and entered into an unpredictable course of self-institution as new polities based on the principle of popular sovereignty. This was a double-tiered and simultaneous process, which involved not just the radical change of political regime but also the definition and redefinition of new sovereign entities that would soon claim their status as autonomous states. The political was at the core of nation-building, so that nation and republic became practically synonymous.

The option for republican forms of government led the nations-in-the-making into a long search for the definition of the basic rules, the main institutions, and the effective practical means of self-government. There were no fixed recipes to this end, and although past and present republican experiences could serve as examples to be avoided or emulated, Spanish Americans had to find their own way to sort out the many challenges posed by their initial choice. From the very beginning, as we have seen, the people played a decisive role in the foundation of the new nations and in the creation and legitimation of political authority. In this regard, the novel republics soon followed the path already taken by their recent predecessors and adopted representative forms of government. The abstract

principle of the sovereignty of the people was therefore materialized through very concrete institutions, such as elections,
that were also common to most other modern polities. Yet
the history of these forms of popular involvement in politics
and of the relationships between the many and the few in
this part of the world show also many differences with other
experiences.

There is no single way of accounting for the peculiarities of
Spanish American republican history, so that rather than pro-
posing an ultimate explanation to the topic of the people in our
republics, in this book I have tried a more limited exercise by
focusing on the political. No doubt other dimensions of social
life may help understand that history, but I argue that politics
itself may offer some clues that are not reducible to any other
instance. In particular, the "invention of the people" and the
forms of inclusion and participation of the many in the life of
the polity followed a peculiar course in Spanish America,
which defined shared, albeit changing, patterns for most of the
nineteenth century and across the region—regardless of the
various ideological trends that alternatively prevailed in each
particular nation, and of the institutional architecture of the
successive regimes.

Those patterns resulted from the actual exercise of politics
in the republic. From the past, colonial legacies left their
marks, but they could scarcely compete with the recent intense
experience of war, with its concomitant effects in terms of the
dislocation of the existing order of things, the organization and
display of military forces, and the widespread mobilization of
the people. From then on, politics involved not just the minority of men who strove to reach positions of power in the new
republics, but it involved large sectors of the population in significant, albeit usually subordinated, ways. This involvement
followed certain established norms and institutional arrange-

ments, and materialized in a series of very concrete practices, which have been described through these pages. These mechanisms favored an intense, sometimes violent, political life. In a context of strong partisan rivalries, whereby competing leaders resorted to all available political means to reach and remain in power, popular mobilization for elections, revolutions, and different sorts of public expressions animated a political dynamic that was highly volatile. Contemporaries were often critical of the resulting political instability, and so they tried different ways to modify that hard fact. Attempts at renouncing to the basic forms of the current republican political life, however, were usually short-lived, and most of the time, these remained a common ground for the successive reforms, regardless of their diverse ideological inspirations. As long as Spanish Americans insisted on this attachment, they could only partially modify the state of things, which was not the result of the republic gone amiss but, rather, of a sustained commitment to some of its founding principles.

A radical turn in this regard took place during the last quarter of the nineteenth century, when new forms of understanding and practicing (republican) politics challenged the ones that had prevailed for several decades. This move was in tune with more global trends in matters republican, with the many adjustments introduced in the United States' political life after the Civil War; the third and definitive adoption, in 1870, of the republic in France—quite different from its previous formulations—and the shift from empire to republic in Brazil, in 1889. These regimes shared with the Spanish American nations the concern for order and stability, an aim not always at hand but that they all sought to achieve in order to avoid the volatility so characteristic of republics in the past.

In this way, what I have called the "republican experiment" came to an end. Spanish American nations kept their republican forms of government, but the rules of the game had changed. And even though change was also at the heart of the process of continuous political experimentation characteristic of the decades following independence—with its share of trial and error, uncertainty and unpredictability—a common political pattern developed and prevailed from the 1820s to the 1870s. This book has tried to identify the main lines of this pattern particularly in regard to a key dimension of republican regimes, the role of the people in the construction and legitimation of power. It has also pointed to the disarticulation of those modes of political participation that announced the beginning of a different type of polity as well as a distinctive "modality of existence of life in common." While in the past, republic and nation as virtual synonyms had been the locus of such common life, in the coming era they parted ways as the "nation" acquired strong cultural connotations and became the ideal incarnation of the community. From then onward and well into the twentieth century, all over the world nationalism became a more substantial, less contingent, reference than the political regime to amalgamate the collective. Thus, Spanish American nations no longer relied on the republic for their communal subsistence; in fact, each of them followed different political trajectories and often alternated republican forms of government with authoritarian regimes that ignored the traditions of self-government so widely cherished in the nineteenth century.

NOTES

Introduction

1. The word *experiment* has several meanings. Here, it is used in the sense made explicit in one of the definitions of the Oxford dictionaries: "A course of action tentatively adopted without being sure of the outcome." http://www.oxforddictionaries.com/definition/english/experiment.

2. Rosanvallon (2003), 14 (see references for chapter 1).

3. Morgan 1988 (see references for chapter 1).

4. This book borrows heavily from a very large number of works on the political history of nineteenth-century Latin America as well as other areas of the world. Rather than including footnotes with long lists of titles, I have chosen to attach a list of references at the end of each chapter. Notes are only used for specific references.

Chapter One. New Republics at Play

1. These first juntas did not explicitly question the colonial authorities in place.

2. The loyalists called them "insurgents," but they called themselves "patriots."

3. Scholars have long associated this situation with the persistence of the corporate imaginaries of the ancien régime, whereby different parts (in this case, territorially grounded) demanded retroversion of sovereignty. More recently, this proliferation of territorial claims has rather been explained resorting to the principles of *ius naturalis* and *ius gentium*, which were invoked in most of the disputes regarding the boundaries of the sovereign claims.

4. Manin 1997.

5. Manin (1997), 170.

Chapter 2. Elections

1. This is a revised and extended version of a text in print included in Eduardo Posada-Carbo and Andrew Robertson, eds. Forthcoming. *The Oxford Handbook of Revolutionary Elections in the Americas, 1800–1910*. Oxford: Oxford University Press.

2. The Cádiz constitution was effective in the territories under the control of Spanish authorities during the "liberal" regimes of 1812 to 1814 and 1820 to 1823. These included the Viceroyalties of New Spain and Peru as well as the recon-

quered areas of the Viceroyalty of New Granada. In the territories controlled by the insurgency, in turn, the introduction of self-government often came hand in hand with electoral procedures of some sort.

3. Rosanvallon (1992), 71 (my translation).

4. The use of the word "vecino" in electoral norms was frequent in the lands where the Cádiz constitution had applied, and it persisted well beyond independence. Thus, for example, all electoral laws of Mexico until 1855 stipulated as a main requisite for potential voters that they be "vecinos" of their locality. The word persisted in different contexts, and probably referred to changing realities, but it somehow kept the implication of belonging to a concrete social setting.

5. These requisites resonate with the limits to citizenship underlined by Rosanvallon for revolutionary France. Rosanvallon 1992.

6. Figures for literacy rates are not very reliable, but available data show a low rate of around 10 to 15 percent for the midcentury in most of Spanish America, with strong differences between urban and rural areas. For the late 1890s, literacy rates remained below 20 percent in Bolivia and Guatemala; between 20 and 30 percent in Mexico, El Salvador, Honduras, and Venezuela; between 30 and 40 percent in Chile, Colombia, Costa Rica, Ecuador, and Paraguay. Argentina's reached 47 percent and Uruguay 59 percent.

7. In Mexico, for example, property and income requirements were introduced in the late 1830s and again in the 1840s, but altogether these were only valid from November 1836 to December 1841 and, again, from June 1843 to August 1846. See Aguilar Rivera 2010.

8. For Europe, see, among others, Garrigou 1992; Rosanvallon 1992; Gueniffey 1993; Tusell 1991; Romanelli 1988; Andreucci 1995; O'Gorman 1996. For the United States, see Keyssar 2000; Peart and Smith 2015.

9. In most of Spanish America, measures to stop the slave trade and to establish freedom of wombs were passed during the first decades after independence. The abolition of slavery, in turn, occurred in Chile, Mexico, and the United Provinces of Central America in the 1820s; in Uruguay in the 1840s; in Colombia, Bolivia, Ecuador, Argentina, Peru, and Venezuela in the 1850s; and in Paraguay in 1869.

10. Manin (1997), 94.

11. Indirect elections prevailed during the entire century in the case of the executive power, with very few exceptions—such as Bolivia in the 1840s and the always cited case of the presidential elections of 1856 in Colombia. For the legislature, in turn, the situation varied greatly. Thus, for example, for several decades after independence, while direct elections for representatives were the rule in the United Provinces of the River Plate and later on in Argentina, as well as in Chile since 1833, in Guatemala since 1838, and in Bolivia between 1839 and 1842, in most other countries representatives were chosen through indirect elections of some kind.

12. The system found a prestigious precedent in several European cases and in the United States' elections for president.

13. Bolivia is an interesting case in point. In 1851, during the presidency of Manuel Belzú, electoral regulations established direct voting for the presidency and the legislature, and confirmed literacy as a requisite for the suffrage. At the same time, an increase in the number of electoral sections that expanded the territorial coverage of voting, as well as a lowering of the *censitaire* restrictions of the suffrage, favored a noticeable enlargement of the turnout. Barragán (2015), 96–97.

14. A classic formulation of this issue for the United States is in Hofstadter 1970.

15. This chronology does not strictly fit evenly to all countries of the region, but it reflects the prevailing trends in the creation of parties as formally recognized and genuine means of political association.

16. The expression "trabajos electorales" (electoral works) was widely used in Latin America to point to a whole range of activities related to elections: the recruitment and mobilization of followers, the organization and control of the potential voters on the day of elections, the performance at the polling stations, the celebrations after a positive result at the polls, or the protests on the face of a lost election, and so forth.

17. The term "faction" was widely used by contemporaries to refer to political groups that presumably did not pursue the common good. Later scholars have frequently resorted to that same word and applied it as an analytical category that allows them to depict the peculiarities of nineteenth-century political associations and differentiate them from twentieth-century parties. The term, however, still carries a strong negative connotation, and rather than a descriptive concept, it remains a value-charged word associated with a propensity to political corruption and divisiveness. See Sabato 2014.

18. Sanders (2004), 128.

19. These figures are, by the way, similar or higher than those found in several European countries in the same period.

20. The National Guard was based on the same principle as the militia: it was an army of citizens (see chapter 3).

21. Mücke (2004), 99–100.

22. Artisans were courted not only by liberals. In Bolivia, Manuel Belzú's nonliberal government displayed a systematic policy of courting artisans as well as other popular groups, both urban and rural. Schelchkov (2011) has portrayed Belzú as "populist, conservative, utopian," p. 286 (my translation).

23. Elections were held at different intervals for the national, the state (in federal republics), and the local levels. Terms of office were generally shorter than today. Often, in elections for collective bodies like legislatures or municipal boards, no surrogates or substitutes were included in the ballot, so that if a member died or resigned, a new election had to be held. No wonder, then, that we may sometimes find places with up to ten elections in a year.

Chapter 3. Citizens in Arms

1. For the US experiences and debates on this topic see, among others, Cress 1984; Carp 1987; Cornell 2006; and Muehlbauer and Ulbrich 2014. For a broader appraisal of the topic of the citizen in arms in the Anglo-Saxon world, see Morgan 1988. A very interesting perspective on the same subject for France is in Rosanvallon 1998.

2. Rabinovich (2013b), 9–10 (my translation). There is no obvious translation into English for *sociedad guerrera*.

3. Frasquet (2007), 119 (my translation).

4. Muehlbauer and Ulbrich (2014), 113 and 127.

5. Thomson (2010), 222 (my translation).

6. "they were joined by the people less appreciated for their education and principles" (my translation). José María Luis Mora, *México y sus revoluciones* (1836), 104–5, cited by Escalante (1992), 206.

7. At least in two cases, Chile and Costa Rica, the national authorities succeeded early on in exerting control over the National Guard, and in turning the institution into an important instrument in the centralization of political power.

8. The opposite was the case in Chile during the 1830s and 1840s, when the central government resorted to the Civic Guard (militia) to consolidate its power and counteract the centrifugal tendencies of the standing army.

9. Méndez (2006), 10.

10. Rabinovich (2013a), 301 (my translation).

11. Wood (2011), 86.

12. Flórez Bolívar and Solano (2011), 103 (my translation).

13. Cited by Wood (2011), 85.

14. Cited by Macías (2014), 164 (my translation).

15. The figures for Mexico are in Fowler (2009), 5; for Argentina, in Malamud (2000), 12; and for Colombia, in Earle (2000), 119.

16. Earle (2000), 3.

17. This understanding of the concept was not peculiar to Spanish America. On the concept of revolution, cf. Williams 1983; Ashcraft 1987; Arendt 1990; Mayer 2000, among others.

18. An interesting comparison between *pronunciamientos* and revolutions in Mexico and Spain is in Thomson 2007.

19. Muehlbauer and Ulbrich (2014), 255.

20. The complete text of the Plan of Tuxtepec is available at http://www .biblioteca.tv/artman2/publish/1876_169/Plan_de_Tuxtepec_lanzado_por _Porfirio_D_az_en_cont_1772.shtml. The words of the San Luis Potosí pronouncement in Cañedo Gamboa (2012) (my translation).

21. Peñaloza's *proclama* is in Halperin Donghi (1980), 232–33; Mitre's Manifesto is in Titto (2009), 212–15 (my translation).

Chapter 4. Public Opinion

1. Baker (1987), 231.

2. Keith Baker has perceptively insisted on the significance of public opinion as a political invention. See Baker (1990), 168.

3. There is a vast body of scholarly works on these topics, a few of which I mention in the references list for this chapter. One of the most influential has been Jürgen Habermas's book on the public sphere. Originally published in 1962, its impact on academic debate outside Germany came much later and generated a prolific discussion that still informs most of the intellectual production in the field.

4. For Spanish America, in his book *Modernidad e independencias*, Guerra argues that the expansion of modern sociability was a key in establishing the preconditions for independence, but in later works he claims that such expansion only took place during the time of the revolutions, and that earlier developments observed for the metropolis had only minor impact in the colonies. Cf. Guerra, Lempérière et al. 1998. For a strong argument regarding the "birth of a public sphere" (with development of new forms of sociability and a periodical press) in the course of the second half of the eighteenth century, see Uribe-Uran 2000.

5. Jacobsen (2005), 278.

6. Figures for Mexico and Peru are in Forment (2003), chapters 11 and 12.

7. Adelman (2006), 185.

8. "Newspapers spring up everywhere," Palti (2003), 191.

9. *La Tribuna*, April 12, 1865 (my translation).

10. *La Tribuna*, April 12, 1865 (my translation).

11. Forment (2003), 385–87 and 405–6.

12. Sabato (2001), 43.

13. Quesada (1883), 75.

14. In 1869, 50 percent of the men and 43 percent of the women could read and write in Buenos Aires, figures that rose to 64 percent and 57 percent by 1887 respectively, well above those of the rest of the country. For overall figures in Spanish America, see chapter 2, note 7.

15. Piccato (2010), 29 and 31.

16. Rabasa (1949), 42 (my translation).

17. *La Tribuna*, September 12, 1875 (my translation).

18. Petitions to the authorities were also a widespread means of expressing the "voice of the people." They came in various forms and followed different protocols. Among the many works that address this topic, see Falcón 2006; Rubio Correa 2003; Reina 1997; Sanders 2014.

19. Piccato (2010), 167, and Habermas (1990), 15. Actually, Habermas argues that Freud and Marx, among others, developed a hybrid discourse that inserted "a genuinely philosophical idea like a detonator into a particular research context." My claim here is less pretentious.

20. Lomnitz (1995), 29.

Chapter 5. The Republican Experiment:
An Essay in Interpretation

1. The expression was coined by James Mill in 1835.

2. Halperin Donghi 1972.

3. There is a long-lasting controversy among scholars regarding the colonial heritage in Latin America.

4. I use here the term *leadership* to refer to the cast of characters who played directive roles in the political life of the republics, both in government positions and in partisan activities. In choosing this descriptive term, I have left aside more precise concepts used by scholars addressing similar problems, such as political class, elites, oligarchy, governing class, notables, and so on. Thus, rather than entering into a conceptual discussion of categories for specific periods and places, I wish to propose some very general features that apply to all.

5. Such was the case, among many others, of Benito Juárez in Mexico, Manuel Belzú in Bolivia, and Agustín Gamarra in Peru, who reached the presidency of their respective countries.

6. Later on, and until today, the term has been applied, by extension, to name political leaders with personal charisma and popular following, both by critics and advocates of that type of leadership.

7. In the case of indigenous groups, there is a specific bibliography that discusses their involvement in the formal political struggles in various periods and places. For an elaborate consideration of this topic see, among many others, Caplan 2010; Mallon 1995; Falcón 2016; Guardino 1995, 1996, 2005; Méndez 2005, 2006; Thomson 1990, 1998, 1999, 2010; Alda Mejías 2002; and the edited volumes by De Jong and Escobar Ohmstede 2016, and Irurozqui 2005.

8. See, for example, the case of the *Sociedad de la Igualdad* in Chile in James Wood (2011), or that of the *Sociedades democráticas* in Colombia in Francisco Gutiérrez (1995).

9. The most consistent exception was that of Paraguay, where Francia ruled as formally designed dictator from 1814 to his death in 1840. He was succeeded then by Carlos Antonio López—first as consul and then as president—until his own death, in 1862, followed by his son Francisco Solano López, who was killed in battle while still in power, toward the end of the War of the Triple Alliance, in 1870.

10. There is a vast bibliography and an ongoing debate on liberalism in Latin America, which I have chosen not to address in this book focused on institutions and practices rather than ideologies.

11. See chapter 2, note 10.

12. *Tributo indígena* was formally eliminated earlier in most countries, but in some of them, it was later reestablished or replaced by a similar type of taxation. Laws abolishing head tax were passed in Argentina, Paraguay, Mexico (only enforced later on), and Chile during the 1810s; in Venezuela and most of the

Central American republics in the 1820s; in Guatemala and Colombia in the 1830s; in Ecuador and Peru in the 1850s; and in Bolivia in the 1870s.

13. *La Tribuna*, July 27, 1873, cited in Sabato 2001.

Epilogue

1. The main exceptions were Brazil, a constitutional monarchy from 1822 to 1889, and Canada, a territory governed by the English until 1867, when it achieved self-rule within the British Empire under the figure of the "dominion." Mexico had a short experience with the monarchy in 1821–23 and later on, from 1864 and 1867.

2. I thank Marcela Ternavasio for her observations in this regard.

INDEX

Adelman, Jeremy, 22
Agustin I, 38, 93
American Revolution, 1–2, 28, 30–31
Argentina: associations in, 138–39,
    141, 142, 144–45; economics in,
    19; constitutions of, 57, 100, 192;
    independence movement in, 31,
    32; militias in, 100–101, 105, 107,
    108, 111–12, 118; population fig-
    ures for, 19; the press in, 149–50,
    153, 154, 155; suffrage in, 57–58,
    60; uprisings and revolutions in,
    113, 117–18; voting practices in,
    67, 70–71, 111–12. *See also* River
    Plate region
armed citizens. *See* militias
Artigas, José Gervasio, 175
artisans, 54, 69–70, 72–73, 96, 110,
    211n22; guilds, 133, 140
associative movement, 134, 137–46,
    156, 158, 184, 194. *See also*
    sociability

Belzú, Manuel, 175, 211n13, 211n22,
    214n5
Bolívar, Simón, 32, 40
Bolivia: constitution of, 39; electoral
    regulations in, 211n13; popula-
    tion figures for, 19; suffrage in, 55
boundary changes, 40
Brazil, 2, 5, 207; constitutional mon-
    archy in, 11, 38, 215n1
Bulnes, Francisco, 111
Bustamante, Carlos María, 92–93

Cabildos Albiertos, 43
Cádiz constitution, 24, 29, 34–35, 38,

209n2; on elections, 50, 52; on
    freedom of the press, 148
Caldera, Rafael, 96
caste system, 19, 37, 172
Catholic Church, 15, 140, 146, 193
caudillos, 174–76, 192, 214n6
centralization, 35, 189, 212n7
Chile: associations in, 142; constitu-
    tion of, 39, 193; independence
    movement in, 31; militias in, 93,
    106–8, 110–11, 212nn7–8; popula-
    tion figures for, 19; the press in,
    154; suffrage in, 53, 55, 57; upris-
    ings and revolutions in, 113; vot-
    ing practices in, 70, 72, 108,
    110–11
citizenship, 52–57, 177–79; armed
    citizenship: *see* militias
civil liberties, 45, 138, 141, 177–78,
    193
Civil War (U.S.), 116, 191, 207
class distinctions. *See* social
    structures
Cochin, Augustin, 136
Colombia: associations in, 142; con-
    stitutions of, 39, 54, 55, 192; eco-
    nomics in, 19; independence
    movement in, 30; indigenous
    population of, 15; militias in, 101,
    107; population figures for, 19;
    suffrage in, 53–54, 57, 58–59; vot-
    ing practices in, 67, 72; wars in,
    113. *See also* Nueva Granada
colonies and metropolis relationship,
    23, 29–33
constitutionalism, 36–37; constitu-
    tional liberalism, 192; constitu-

A NOTE ON THE TYPE

THIS BOOK has been composed in Miller, a Scotch Roman typeface designed by Matthew Carter and first released by Font Bureau in 1997. It resembles Monticello, the typeface developed for The Papers of Thomas Jefferson in the 1940s by C. H. Griffith and P. J. Conkwright and reinterpreted in digital form by Carter in 2003.

Pleasant Jefferson ("P. J.") Conkwright (1905–1986) was Typographer at Princeton University Press from 1939 to 1970. He was an acclaimed book designer and AIGA Medalist.

The ornament used throughout this book was designed by Pierre Simon Fournier (1712–1768) and was a favorite of Conkwright's, used in his design of the *Princeton University Library Chronicle*.